Kabbalah for Teens

D1314429

Kabbalah
for Teens

LOUIS BELMONT

The Tycher Library
in the
Mankoff Center for Jewish Learning

CITADEL PRESS
Kensington Publishing Corp.
www.kensingtonbooks.com

CITADEL PRESS BOOKS are published by

Kensington Publishing Corp.
850 Third Avenue
New York, NY 10022

Copyright © 2005 Louis Belmont

All rights reserved. No part of this book may be reproduced in any form or by any means without the prior written consent of the publisher, excepting brief quotes used in reviews.

All Kensington titles, imprints, and distributed lines are available at special quantity discounts for bulk purchases for sales promotions, premiums, fund-raising, educational, or institutional use. Special book excerpts or customized printings can also be created to fit specific needs. For details, write or phone the office of the Kensington special sales manager: Kensington Publishing Corp., 850 Third Avenue, New York, NY 10022, attn: Special Sales Department; phone 1-800-221-2647.

CITADEL PRESS and the Citadel logo are Reg. U.S. Pat. & TM Off.

First printing: April 2005

10 9 8 7 6 5 4 3 2 1

Printed in the United States of America

Library of Congress Control Number: 2004116397

ISBN 0-8065-2588-6

Contents

Kabbalah for Teens

Introduction

The title of this book—*Kabbalah for Teens*—would have shocked the ancient scholars and teachers of this secret mystical tradition. In simplest terms, Kabbalah is a profound way of interpreting the Bible and its relevance to our lives as individuals, as well as the place of our species in the universe as a whole. This may seem innocent enough, but for many centuries it was thought to be dangerous for the average person to start thinking too much. Thus, all sorts of qualifications were required before a student could begin Kabbalistic studies, and among these qualifications was an age limit: not eighteen or twenty-one, but *forty*. The tools and teachings of Kabbalah were considered so powerful that people had to be well into middle age before the lessons could even be approached.

Whatever the reasons may have been in the past, the idea of prohibiting the study of Kabbalah certainly has no place in the modern world. On the contrary, Kabbalistic teachings are so insightful, compassionate, and empowering that they need to be brought to as many people as possible in the shortest possible time. *Kabbalah for Teens* is a step in that direction. Its purpose is to present authentic Kabbalistic teachings in a format that retains the flavor of the ancient texts, while also showing their application to today's world.

Regarding this, one point needs to be made at the beginning—and we'll return to it repeatedly throughout the book. *Kabbalah isn't easy and it isn't supposed to be easy.* The writings of Kabbalah aren't particularly easy to understand, nor are they easy to live up to in our everyday lives. This is as it should be because the effort required is an essential element of the teachings themselves. We must earn the wisdom that Kabbalah can bring into our lives. No one—not even God himself—can just *give* it to us. God, after all, gave us a paradise in the Garden of Eden, and we got ourselves banished. Now we have the challenge (and the opportunity) of earning our way back in.

In this sense, difficulty is not a bad word in Kabbalisitc teachings. Difficulty is the medium through which you attain understanding and through which you grow. Therefore, you must be prepared to confront some of these difficulties in this book—which actually aren't that difficult. They're just somewhat different from what you may find in other books or from what you're used to in movies or television.

Specifically, the teachings of Kabbalah deliberately leave out the explanatory material that you might be expecting to find. Kabbalah is not a strictly logical system of thought. Many "empty spaces" need to be filled by its readers and students, or perhaps the empty spaces were just meant to be ignored. Here's an example: In chapter 5, you will read about two men looking up at the top of a mountain. Both of them see a huge pillar of fire. But when they arrive on the mountaintop, there seems to be no fire of any kind. In fact, neither of the men even mentions the pillar of fire. Neither of them asks, "What's going on here? Where's the fire?" Needless to say, if this were to happen in a modern science fiction film, you might see it as a glaring error on the part of the scriptwriter and the director. But the ancient Kabbalists were not worried about tying all the loose ends together. Their focus was on the deeper meaning of the stories—and if that meant fudging some of the realistic details, they did so without hesitation. So be prepared.

As you begin your encounter with Kabbalah, try to see the obstacles as "mind expanding" rather than just confusing. Start with the idea that the creators of these teachings "knew what they were doing," even if they went about it in a way that shifts the burden of explanation from them to us. When you do this, you will begin to experience a truly Kabbalistic point of view. This will help you to understand what you read here, which in turn can benefit you hugely in every area of your life.

Life Is Very Complicated

If you disagree with that statement, you probably have no need for this book. But the chances are that you do feel there are moments when your life seems difficult and even out of control. Sometimes those difficult times last only a few moments or a few days. Sometimes they last for years.

Right now, if you're between the ages of thirteen and twenty, you're probably well aware of how complex your life is becoming. The purpose of this book is to reveal the basic order that's hidden within the daily complexity. By the time you reach the last page, you'll have learned a completely new way of looking at your life— and you'll have gained some powerful tools for making your life more productive, more successful, and a lot more fun.

This new way of looking at things is not the product of any single philosopher or teacher or wise man or woman. Instead, it's based on a spiritual system—not a religion—that has existed for many thousands of years. That system is called *Kabbalah*, a Hebrew word whose literal meaning is *to receive*.

Over the centuries, the teachings of Kabbalah passed from spiritual masters to a select number of students. Often these masters and students were the descendants of earlier Kabbalists. Sometimes, according to Kabbalistic teachings, they were even reincarnations of them, and a few, such as Rabbi Shimon bar Yochai (author of the mystical book known as the Zohar), were said to be reincarnations of great biblical figures such as Moses and King David.

The Zohar

The Zohar is one of the world's great mystical books. Everything about it is mysterious, including its authorship. Today most scholars believe that Spanish Kabbalist Rabbi Moses de Leon composed the Zohar in the thirteenth century. Rabbi de Leon, however, asserted that he had copied the Zohar from an ancient manuscript ascribed to Rabbi Shimon bar Yochai, who lived under the Roman occupation of what is now Israel, two centuries after the birth of Christ.

The content of the Zohar is simple enough on the physical level, but very complex philosophically. It concerns the travels of a group of friends, led by Rabbi Shimon bar Yochai, who discuss the Bible and occasionally have adventures. They meet a humble donkey driver, for example, who turns out to be the reincarnation of a famous mystical teacher. But as soon as they realize this, the donkey driver disappears into thin air.

Over the centuries, the Zohar has sometimes played an important role in Jewish spiritual practice, while at other times it has been ignored or even deliberately suppressed. Fifty years ago an English translation of the Zohar was almost impossible to find, but today there are several different translations to choose from. If you are interested in learning more about Kabbalah, you need to investigate this amazing work, which is usually published in several volumes. You may not understand very much at first, but don't worry—you can keep studying the Zohar for the rest of your life!

To prevent them from falling into the wrong hands, most of the Kabbalistic lessons were never written down. As we have said, anyone under the age of forty was banned from even beginning Kabbalistic studies, under the threat of going blind if the prohibition was violated. These strict regulations were in place because the Kabbalistic masters genuinely believed that the world as a whole was not ready to absorb these teachings. It was thought that people needed simple religious rituals, rather than powerful insights that could widen their horizons and encourage them to change their lives radically.

Today the situation is reversed. Kabbalah may indeed have been ahead of its time. Perhaps there was justification for keeping it hidden in societies in which any desire for self-improvement was severely punished by the authorities. But things change. The world (that includes you!) is ready for this knowledge, and when you begin to understand Kabbalah and to use its spiritual tools, you will see why this is true.

As you begin to explore this ancient body of knowledge, you'll find words, ideas, and viewpoints that are very different from anything you're used to. After all, these are mystical teachings from Eastern Europe and the Middle East, dating from medieval times and earlier. It would certainly be possible to present Kabbalah in a way that would be very difficult to understand—and it may be that some people actually want Kabbalah to be difficult. Perhaps this makes the self-appointed guardians of this knowledge seem more important to themselves. But Kabbalah can also be taught as a very practical and down-to-earth way of looking at the world. That's the direction we'll be taking here. Still, you can be sure that the ideas you'll find here are indeed authentic teachings of the Kabbalistic masters. They're just presented in a way that they will be of maximum use to readers such as yourself, in the world you live in right now.

Let's look at an example of exactly what this means.

A girl named Nicole was looking for an after-school job. She went to the mall near her home and filled out an application at a store that sold clothes and accessories for young people like herself. The clothes in the store were on the expensive side, but they were also fun and slightly funky—which was exactly how

Nicole liked to see herself. A few days later, she was very excited when she received a phone call to come in for an interview. She carefully dressed in an outfit that mirrored the things she would be selling. Getting dressed like this to go to work a few times each week was going to be great. Maybe, as an employee, she would even get discounts on purchases from the store.

Nicole's interview with the store manager went great, at least at first. She asked Nicole some interesting questions about the kinds of clothes and jewelry she liked to wear, and she seemed very interested in Nicole's responses. They got along so well that Nicole was sure she was going to be hired. She was sure, that is, until the manager asked her something that took her completely by surprise.

"I'd like you to take a typing test," said the store manager.

Nicole hesitated, but managed to keep smiling. Why should she have to take a typing test? Wasn't this supposed to be a sales job? And most important, she couldn't type!

"Is something the matter?" asked the manager. Apparently Nicole's smile was starting to look a bit frozen.

"No, nothing's the matter. Not really," Nicole said. "But I guess I don't see why I need a typing test to sell skirts and blouses."

The manager nodded. "It does seem kind of silly," she agreed, "but it's just company policy. In order to come on board, everyone has to take a typing test, regardless of his or her job. I had to take one when I was hired, and so did the person who hired me."

"Well, it seems sort of senseless."

"I agree with you. Maybe it is senseless," said the manager, now just slightly impatient. "But like I said, it's company policy. So let's not make it into something bigger than it has to be."

Suddenly Nicole was no longer smiling. It seemed to her that people were always trying to get her to do senseless things, whether it was her parents, her teachers, or even her friends. For some reason, she had thought having a job in the adult world would be different. But now it looked like it would just be more of the same.

"I just don't see why I have to take a typing test in order to sell clothes," she said again, surprised at the angry note that had suddenly crept into her voice.

"Nicole, I don't really have to explain why you have to take a typing test. But you do have to take one if you want to work in this store."

"Well, maybe I don't want to work in this store."

"Apparently not. Have a nice day."

The next day, when Nicole told some of her friends about what had happened, one word seemed to come up repeatedly in what they told her. That word was "wrong." Nicole had behaved in the wrong way. What she said was wrong. There was something wrong in pretty much everything she did. Nicole didn't even bother to tell her parents about what happened, because she was sure they'd just tell her the same thing. If they asked about the interview, Nicole decided, she'd just say that the store wasn't hiring after all.

If we look at Nicole's interview from a Kabbalistic viewpoint, we, too, might conclude that she behaved wrongly—but the word wrong would mean something different from what Nicole's friends and family intended.

According to Kabbalistic teachings, actions are "right" when they bring us closer to the happiness that God intends for us. Our actions are wrong when they move us in the opposite direction.

So Kabbalah tells us that right and wrong are a matter of recognizing your true self-interest, of seeing what is really best for you, and of acting in a way that will bring that into your life.

It's not about God judging you or finding you innocent or guilty. It's about really knowing what will make you happy based on what you want and need right now in all areas of your life. Once you recognize what you want and need, it just makes good sense to act accordingly.

This combination of knowledge and action is basic to Kabbalistic wisdom. But it's not the true foundation of that wisdom—which, in fact, needs to be made clear right here at the start. As you first read it, you may find it hard to relate to what it says or what it seems to be saying. Largely, this is because Kabbalah is not an abstract philosophy. It's best understood through stories and real-life situations, which is what you'll find in the pages that follow.

But first, there are fundamental principles that you'll need to keep in mind as you begin to connect with the wisdom of Kabbalah, not just in this book, but in your life as you live it every day. This fundamental wisdom can be most clearly expressed in three parts, although the three are inseparable. As you become more familiar with them, you'll see that they're actually just different ways of looking at the same thing.

First, you must completely and absolutely reject the role of victim anywhere in your life. You must stop blaming others for anything that happens to you. You must refuse to feel sorry for yourself in any situation, no matter how painful or unjust the situation may seem. In fact, you must see the injustice itself as an opportunity to assert your rejection of victimhood, no matter what!

The second point is really the mirror image of the first. At the same time as Kabbalah teaches us to reject victimhood, it also teaches us to accept and embrace the idea that *we ourselves and nobody else* are completely responsible for whatever happens to us, for whatever comes into our lives. Whatever problems or obstacles you are facing right now are nothing but the blossoming of seeds you yourself planted—and you must accept this in order to grow into the totally fulfilled and happy person you are intended to be.

Third, you must extend your responsibility beyond yourself to the lives of others. You must come to see how, by being a better person yourself, you can make others better. What's more, it's your responsibility to do so. Kabbalah teaches that there is no such thing as mere "self-help." No one can become a better or a happier person without intention and action toward making other people happy also.

Remember: *None of this is easy, and it's not supposed to be easy.* You are not here in the world in order to stay within your comfort zone. You are here to grow to the very limit of your soul—and even beyond the limit, as the great sages of the past have done. Once again, this is not easily understood when it is presented in abstract terms. It will only become clear through specific applications in the "real world." In this book, the real world may refer to the world of the past, which has come down to us through the tales and legends of Kabbalah. Or it may also mean the modern environment of school, of teachers, of parents, sports, and of seemingly impossible amounts of homework. Only the scenery changes. The lessons are the same and so are the spiritual forces that are working to change your life for the better.

Ten Rungs of the Ladder

Throughout nature, living things behave by instinct. If a squirrel arrives at the base of a tree, the squirrel will instinctively begin to climb. It's not because it knows what it'll find in the branches of the tree; it's just its nature to move from a low point to a higher one. In fact, the squirrel doesn't even need a tree to demonstrate this characteristic. It'll also instinctively climb stairways, slanted boards, or anything that will take it from down to up.

Kabbalah teaches that human beings have this same climbing instinct, but it expresses itself spiritually rather than physically. A great teacher of Kabbalah, for example, compared our lives to a person standing at the base of a ladder that extends high into the clouds. The person begins to climb, not because he or she knows what will be found at the top, but because climbing is the person's natural desire. As one climbs from one rung to the next, this desire only grows stronger. The higher one goes, the higher one wants to get.

Kabbalah teaches that an invisible ladder with ten rungs can lead us to God. In order to climb from one rung to the next, we need to connect to very specific forms of energy, and as we do so, we become wiser and more joyful. Our nature becomes less dominated by the worries and fears that characterize many people's lives and more like the peace and fulfillment that is the essence of God.

This book will introduce you to the ten rungs of the Kabbalistic ladder—that is, to the ten forms of energy and wisdom that you can use to gain understanding, find solutions to problems, and improve your life. In Hebrew, the rungs of the ladder are called *sefirot*, plural of *sefirah*. A literal translation of *sefirah* is difficult to render, but the closest English word is probably *emanation*—something that's sent forth or radiated. In this case, it's the wisdom and love that radiates from God.

Kabbalah teaches that we can never really know the true nature of God, who exists beyond even the highest of the Sefirot. But we can draw closer to God and to the happiness that He intends for us. In fact, it is our nature to do so. We can make that ascent through knowledge of the ten Sefirot and through actions based on that knowledge.

As you'll see, Kabbalah is not about becoming a saint or an angel. It's really a set of tools for making your life better in every way. It's not theory, it's action. So let's get started.

—⁓—

The Sefirot

For thousands of years, the great teachers of Kabbalah have referred to this diagram as "The Tree of Life." It depicts the ten Sefirot and the relationship among them. The diagram is like a model of the genetic structure of human life—it depicts the DNA of the human soul. But it is even more than that. It expresses the energy makeup of the whole universe, for Kabbalah teaches that the essence of every human being and all of Creation are one and the same. Because of this, the Tree of Life and the ten Sefirot are both within us and at the same time all around us.

Throughout this book, we'll discuss each of the ten Sefirot in detail, and we'll see how each plays a very active part in your life every day. For now, here's a brief look at each of the emanations and the unique energies they express.

Malchut ("Kingdom" in Hebrew)

This is world we live in now. It includes all physical reality, along with the thoughts and feelings we experience in our daily lives. Malchut is God's presence in the material world. We may not be aware of this presence, and many people are not aware of it. But there are also people who see God everywhere and in everything. This level of awareness is the true fulfillment of the human soul, and Kabbalah exists to help us reach that awareness.

Ysod ("Foundation")

Ysod is the union of the other Sefirot as they make the transition into the physical world. It's the bridge between our level of being and the levels of the Upper World. It's like the volume control on a CD player that allows us to hear the music of an orchestra at a level that's comfortable for our ears.

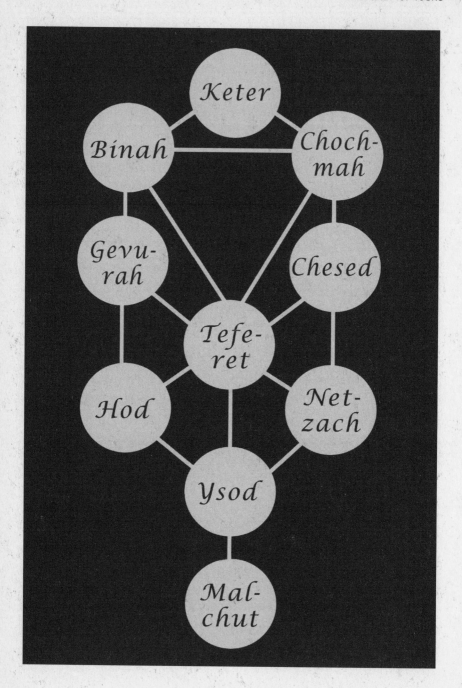

Hod ("Awe")

Hod is the expression of honesty, self-knowledge, and truth.

Netzach ("Victory")

Netzach is the sacred power of creation, through which the universe has come into being. It's the victory over the forces of negativity and chaos that makes everything else possible.

Gevurah ("Judgment")

Gevurah is the energy of justice and restraint. When we perform actions in the physical world, Gevurah brings the consequences of those actions into being.

Chesed ("Kindness," "Mercy")

Chesed represents the purest form of love—a person's ability to give and to share while asking nothing in return.

Teferet ("Balance")

Teferet represents balance and resolution between the powers of kindness and judgment.

Binah ("Knowledge")

Binah is the power of divine intelligence that God applied in creating the universe, as well as the Sefirot themselves.

Chochmah ("Wisdom")

Chochmah is the more abstract knowledge that is the starting point from which God's emanations begin to take form.

Keter ("Crown")

Here all the energies of God's being reside in perfect balance, ready to separate themselves in the lower nine Sefirot.

If these brief descriptions of the Sefirot seem to leave many questions unanswered, don't worry. The rest of this book will be devoted to explaining them in the context of your everyday life while also remaining true to the timeless lessons of the Kabbalistic masters. The lessons you will learn here are much more than ancient artifacts. They are tools you can start using right now to make your life become happier, richer, and hugely less stressful.

In the following ten chapters, we'll look at each of the ten Sefirot in several different ways. Each chapter begins with a traditional tale that reveals the meaning and power of the specific Sefirah. Most of these tales originated in Eastern Europe during the nineteenth century, during a flowering of interest in the mystical aspects of Judaism; others are from the Bible itself. Each of these stories is followed by another that is set in the modern world and deals with the same theme. Finally, the chapters close with a discussion of the particular Sefirah and its place in life as we know it today.

CHAPTER ONE

Malchut

The Kingdom of This World

In the Garden of Eden that God created for Adam and Eve, everything was perfect. There was no suffering, no pain, no illness, and no hunger. Things could have stayed like that forever if Adam and Eve had obeyed God's command not to eat the fruit of a forbidden tree. But they disobeyed that command. A serpent tempted them to eat the fruit, and as a result, they were banished from Paradise.

Over the centuries, there have been many attempts to understand why God created a tree with luscious fruit, and then told Adam and Eve not to eat from it. Why did he create the tree in the first place? Some scholars have said that God was deliberately setting a trap for Adam and Eve so that he could exile them from Eden.

In fact, there is truth to this interpretation. But according to Kabbalistic teaching it does not go far enough. Kabbalah teaches that God banished Adam and Eve from Paradise so that they could earn their way back in. But as to how they could accomplish that feat— well, they would have to figure that out for themselves!

The two stories that follow illustrate this principle: The first one is based on an episode from the Bible, in the twenty-ninth chapter of the book of Genesis. The second story was written by a girl named Cathy, who lives in the suburbs of a large midwestern city. Read

Bible or Torah?

The Hebrew word *Torah* derives from a word meaning "teaching" or "true teaching." Strictly speaking, the Torah is the first five books of what we now call the Bible: Genesis, Exodus, Leviticus, Numbers, and Deuteronomy. In a more general sense, Torah has come to mean the entire body of Jewish wisdom, including all the books of the Bible and the commentaries on them. A Torah is also a parchment scroll in which the first five books of the Bible have been inscribed in Hebrew, according to a carefully followed ancient procedure. In this book, the word "Torah" generally refers to the Bible as a whole, but not to the commentaries or the scroll.

these two stories and the commentary that follows to understand why things sometimes seem so complicated in this world and why the complications themselves are actually opportunities in disguise.

The following story is adapted from the biblical book of Genesis. Like all great love stories, it has some surprising twists and turns.

The Marriage of Jacob and Rachel

Abraham was the father, or patriarch, of the Jewish people. For many years he and his wife Sarah were unable to have children, but when they were very old—almost a hundred years old, according to the Bible—Sarah gave birth to a son. They named him Isaac.

Isaac grew up and married a woman named Rebecca. They became the parents of twin boys named Esau and Jacob. Esau was tough and athletic. He loved to spend his time hunting in the fields.

Jacob was more thoughtful and sensitive. Throughout the boys' youth, Isaac felt closer to Esau, while Rebecca was closer to Jacob.

Years passed, and Isaac began to grow old and weak. Eventually he became blind. Rebecca was worried that Esau, who was his father's favorite, would receive Isaac's blessing and inheritance. So she came up with a plan to deceive her husband.

Since Isaac was now blind, Rebecca knew that he recognized his sons by touch. Esau's skin was rough and hairy, but Jacob's was smoother. So Rebecca killed a goat and allowed its skin to dry in the sun. Then she covered Jacob's hands and arms with the rough-textured hide. She told Jacob to bring Isaac some of his favorite food for the noontime meal. Rebecca knew that Isaac would be so happy about this that he would bestow the inheritance on Jacob then and there—especially since Isaac would think he was giving the inheritance to Esau!

The trick worked perfectly. But when Esau found out what had happened, he was furiously angry. He wanted to kill Jacob. Since Jacob knew that his brother was indeed capable of murdering him, he immediately ran away.

Without a specific destination in mind, Jacob traveled eastward—toward the country where his grandfather Abraham had been born, and where his father, Isaac, had met Rebecca. In the back of his mind, Jacob also hoped to find a wife with whom he could start a family and build a new life away from Esau and the danger that his brother represented.

One day Jacob came to a well in the fields outside a small town. There were some shepherds at the well watering their sheep, and Jacob asked them what the town was called. "It's called Haran," they told him. Jacob was very excited to hear this because, after all, he still had some blood relations in the country of his grandfather.

"You must know my uncle!" exclaimed Jacob to the shepherds. "His name is Laban, and he lives in Haran."

"We know him very well," one of the shepherds replied. "And look! Here comes Laban's daughter Rachel, with a flock of his sheep!"

Jacob turned and saw a beautiful young woman coming toward them. Instantly, he fell deeply in love with her. In fact, the sudden infusion of energy that he experienced gave him superhuman strength. Without even thinking about it, Jacob moved a huge stone that covered the entrance to the well. It usually required several men to move the stone, but Jacob did it all by himself.

Then he smiled at Rachel. "Now you can water your sheep," he said, and then he kissed her.

Rachel, of course, was surprised, but Jacob explained that they were actually related. Together they went back to Rachel's home. When she told her father that she had met a long lost relative, Laban was overjoyed, and he embraced Jacob happily.

"My sister Rebecca is your mother," he declared. Laban hadn't known until now that he even had a nephew.

Jacob stayed with Laban's family for several weeks. He helped with the hard work of living in the desert. Finally Laban said to him, "I appreciate all you've done, and I hope you'll stay a long time. But I don't expect you to work for nothing. What kind of wages do you want?"

Jacob didn't hesitate. He had actually been expecting a conversation like this with Laban. He said, "I love Rachel and I want to marry her. I'll stay here and work for seven years if you'll let her be my bride."

Actually, Laban had also been planning for this conversation, and he had been expecting Jacob to say exactly what he'd said. "I'd prefer for you to marry Rachel rather than anyone else," Laban said. "So I accept your proposition." But first, Jacob would have to work for Laban for seven years. So Jacob worked for Laban for seven years, and his love for Rachel was so strong that the years seemed like only a few days. At last the time for the marriage began to draw near.

This is how marriages were arranged in ancient times. Often they were arranged very far in advance, and often the bride did not have much say in the matter. But in this case, Rachel had been very happy about the prospect of being Jacob's wife. Then she suddenly appeared to grow worried.

"What's wrong?" Jacob asked.

"Well, I'm concerned about Leah—" Rachel began.

Leah was Rachel's older sister. She was not as beautiful as Rachel was, but, after all, Rachel was one of the most beautiful women in the land. Jacob had not really paid too much attention to Leah. But now Rachel seemed very worried about her.

"Jacob, there's something I need to tell you," she said. "I'm worried that my father might somehow try to trick you into marrying Leah instead of me. You see, he wants to have his older daughter married off first, as is the custom."

Hearing this, Jacob could hardly keep from laughing. "How could such a thing possibly happen?" he said.

"I know it sounds unlikely, but Laban can be a very deceptive person. Listen, here's what I think we should do. Let's have a secret word. Before the ceremony in the wedding hall, quietly ask me for the word. When I give it to you, you'll know it's me and not Leah."

Jacob still found this all very difficult to believe, but he saw no harm in going along with what Rachel said. So they agreed on a secret word, and preparations for the marriage began.

Perhaps Jacob should have taken Rachel's warning more seriously. In those days, weddings took place with the bride's face covered by a veil. When the ceremony began, it occurred to Jacob that there actually was the possibility of deception. "It's a good thing Rachel came up with the secret word trick," he thought to himself—and leaning close to his veiled bride, he asked her for the word. When she repeated it without hesitation, Jacob was reassured and the ceremony continued to its end.

But when the bride removed her veil, Jacob got a big surprise. His new wife was not Rachel, but Rachel's sister Leah! Furious with anger, Jacob ran up to Laban. "You tricked me! You promised me Rachel, but you gave me Leah instead!"

"You see," Laban replied, "it's the custom in our country to have the older daughter get married before the younger. I know you're upset, but that's just the way we do things around here." And he smiled sadly, as if to say, "There's really nothing I can do about it." Now Jacob turned to Rachel. Grabbing her by the arm, he quickly took her outside so that they cold talk in private.

"Why did you trick me?" Jacob shouted at her. "That whole business with the secret word was a lie! You and your sister had it all worked out from the beginning!"

But to Jacob's surprise, Rachel was not in the least bit sorry. "Well, it looks like the deceiver has been deceived! How did your brother Esau feel after you dressed up in goatskin to fool your father? Sometimes people have to do things that aren't exactly straightforward, but it all works out for the best."

"But why did you have to deceive me like this?" Jacob protested. "I thought we loved each other."

"Oh, we do love each other," Rachel said. "But I love Leah too—and anyway, love isn't the only reason people do things in this world. If I had gotten married before Leah, no one would have ever wanted her, and she knows it. She's been crying so much that I'm worried she might be hurting her eyes. Furthermore, she's really a very wonderful person. Once you get to know her, I think you'll learn to love her almost as much as you love me. And you do love me, don't you?"

Jacob stared at Rachel for a long moment. Though he was still angry with her, he also continued to find her irresistible. "Yes," he admitted. "I can't help it. I do love you even now. But now I'm married to Leah and not to you."

Rachel nodded. "Yes, that's right. But maybe if you talked to my father about the situation, something can be worked out. I certainly hope so, because our love is a beautiful thing." And then she kissed him.

—⚏—

Jacob went back into the wedding hall and took Laban aside. "I still love Rachel and I still want to marry her," Jacob said. "Is there any way that can happen?"

Laban looked thoughtful. "Well, in our country men are permitted to have more than one wife, and there are many who believe that two wives are better than one. I've got an idea! If you agree to work for me for another seven years, I'll let you marry Rachel right away!"

And that's what happened. Jacob married Rachel, and then he worked for his uncle for seven more years. And his love for Rachel was so strong that he would have worked much longer, even for a hundred years.

Waiting, and impatience with waiting, is still a part of life. Jacob learned to wait—and work—before he could marry Rachel. The girl in the following story learns a similar lesson.

My Sister and I

I started gymnastics when I was just four years old, and I've always had a talent for it. By the time I was a sophomore in high school, I was one of the best girl gymnasts in my state. In every meet I've been in, I've taken home at least one medal.

Our final competition of the season was one of my best efforts—I won first place in floor exercise, which involved spectacular acrobatics such as forward and back flips. My parents congratulated my coach, my coach congratulated my parents, and everyone congratulated me. Even Rita, my younger sister, gave me a smile.

How can I describe Rita? When I was very young, I used to hear people say that she was "retarded"—even my parents used that word. Now they say she's "developmentally challenged." Whatever it's called, Rita doesn't seem to understand a lot of what's going on. Sometimes I think that might actually be a good thing, because she doesn't know what she's missing. She doesn't know that I'm doing so well in gymnastics, and she doesn't realize how proud my parents are of me. Rita just seems happy all the time. She never changes.

After I had won the medal for floor exercise, my coach asked Mom and Dad to meet her in her office. I stayed outside in the hallway with Rita. When the meeting was over, my parents walked out of the office looking happy, but also somewhat stunned. During the ride home, I found out why. The coach had given them a brochure for an Olympics-training gymnastics camp in Duluth, Minnesota. She told them that I might be good enough to be in the Olympics if I received the best possible training. But the only way I would be eligible for the Olympics tryout program would be to take this summer camp.

I was so thrilled to hear about all this! "That's great!" I said. "I can't wait to go!"

But my father didn't seem nearly as enthusiastic. "That camp is very expensive, Cathy. We've already planned to send Rita to a special day camp this summer, which also costs a lot of money."

I couldn't believe my ears. Didn't they understand about Rita? If she skipped her camp, she'd just keep on being happy, like always. She'd never know what she was missing. But if I didn't go to the camp in Minnesota, I would never be able to compete in the Olympics!

"Can't Rita wait another year?" I said. "I can't wait. I'm already fourteen!"

They didn't answer, which I knew was a bad sign. How could my own parents not care about this tremendous opportunity? They'd been around gymnastics long enough to know that you've missed your chance if you're not in the Olympics tryout program by the time you're sixteen.

At dinner that night, I did my "I'm not hungry" thing. They hate it when I don't eat. Why? They're scared I might get an eating dis-order—and I was just angry enough to try one!

My mother looked worried. "I made a roast and you're not hungry?" she said.

"Rita can have my food," I said sarcastically.

My father looked sad. "Sometimes I wonder what we're going to do with you, Cathy," he said.

"I know what you can do! Send me to the gymnastics camp!" Then I stood up and marched out of the dining room.

That night I sneaked into the kitchen to get some cold pot roast. To my surprise, Rita was in the kitchen too. It was almost as if she had been waiting for me.

"I don't have to go to camp," she said. "You should be the one to go."

Wow, that sounded great! "Thanks, Rita!" I said. "Tell that to mom and dad in the morning, okay?"

"Okay."

"You'll remember?"

"Sure."

And she did tell them too. They listened carefully, and to my surprise, they seemed to like what they heard. "Do you really want to go to the gymnastics camp?" my father asked.

"*Yes!*"

Then my mom took over. "I think we've come up with a way for you to attend that camp after all."

I was almost crying for joy! I hugged both of them and told them how much I loved them and how much this meant to me—and Rita didn't even have to cover for me. I could hardly wait to tell all my friends.

I was just about to reach for the phone when I noticed that my mother was looking at me very seriously. "I said there was a way for you to go, if you really want it. But there's something you have to do in order to make that happen."

"Really? Name it, Mom. Just tell me what you want from me. No problem!"

Well, I asked for it, and I got it. My mother explained that she had gotten an e-mail message from the director of Rita's camp. It seemed that some of the experienced counselors were unavailable that summer. The parents of prospective campers were being asked if they know anyone who might be interested.

"It's a three-week job," my father said. "I will pay enough for your flight to Minnesota, with a little left over to help cover the cost of the gymnastics camp itself."

A strange feeling came over me. It was as if they thought I understood what they were talking about, and maybe I thought I understood it, but I really couldn't believe it. Were they trying to tell me that I should work at a day camp for mentally handicapped kids? Rita was my sister, my own flesh and blood—but others? Plus, I'm not the "teacher" type. Not everyone is suited for that kind of thing.

However, my parents informed me that unless I took this job, I would absolutely and positively *not* be attending the gymnastics camp. This was so unfair! I felt as if they were holding a gun to my head, as if they were pushing me toward the edge of a cliff. But I could tell they were very serious. Unfair as it seemed, this was the chance I had to live out my Olympic dream. So, with tears streaming down my face, I agreed. Of course, Rita was overjoyed. She shouted "Yea!" I wanted to die.

Early that summer, on the first day of camp, Mom drove Rita and me to the park where the camp was being held. I'd had a brief meeting with the camp directors during the spring. Now, along with the other counselors, I was brought into a dingy meeting room in the park recreation center. This would be our orientation. We were given some basic instructions about dealing with mentally disabled kids, and we looked at a schedule of our activities for the camp's three weeks. It seemed simple enough. I would be loosely supervised by a head counselor. Otherwise, I would be helping a small group of kids with art, sports, and singing. I was also told to keep a journal describing the progress of the campers, as well as my own feelings about working with these "special" kids. At the end of the camp session, copies of the journal would be given to the campers, to be read by their parents, most likely.

I was assigned to a group of six kids, and Rita was one of them. She was so happy—but she was always happy. I sat under a tree with my group and showed them a book with pictures of animals. As I identified each animal, the kids were supposed to repeat what I said. The funny thing was, it wasn't that easy! I didn't know what a few of the animals were, so I gave them imaginary names. One was a "shmengie" and another was a "schvike." The kids couldn't believe how great this was, especially Rita. She laughed and hit her little fists, which was what she always did when she was excited.

At one point we were looking at a picture of a pig. (I knew that one!) "The pig lives in a sty," I said. "He says oink."

Suddenly, before the kids could repeat this, a boy named Alan burst out laughing. "The pig lives in a sty," Alan said. "He says oy!" Actually, I thought that was amazingly funny. In our Jewish family everyone was always saying "oy," and I had even taught some of my Christian friends to say it. But none of the other kids understood that Alan had been making a joke. They just thought he had misunderstood what I said. So now they laughed too—but they were laughing at Alan, rather than with him. But not Rita. She knew that they were making fun of Alan.

She shouted. "Stop laughing! Alan is trying very hard!"

I was astounded. I had never seen her act this way. In fact, I could hardly remember a time when she had not had a smile on her face. The kids fell silent. "Say you are sorry to Alan," Rita told them.

"I'm sorry," they said in unison.

We looked at some more pictures. Out of the corner of my eye, I noticed that Alan had begun rocking back and forth. At first I ignored it, but he kept going faster and faster. Was this something he did when he felt excited, like Rita hitting her fists? By now he was moving so fast that everyone noticed. One of the other boys piped up. "He's gotta go!" the boy said.

I was momentarily puzzled. "Gotta go?"

Then Rita crawled toward me and whispered in my ear, "He's gotta go to the bathroom! You'd better take him!"

"Oh. Okay!"

Alan and I rushed toward the bathrooms in the recreation center. I did wonder whether I should be leaving all those kids under a tree in the park. But this was a safe suburban area, and I had not been told anything about this. So off we went. When Alan and I returned to the group, we found the head counselor standing there, looking very concerned. She took me aside.

"Never leave them alone!" she said in a sharp whisper. "Bring them over to another group if you have to leave! Even for a moment!"

"Sorry, it won't happen again."

"Please—no more mistakes like that, Cathy. They're completely dependent on you."

She walked off, and I went back to the kids. She could have fired me on the spot! I'd have blown my chance to go to gymnastics camp! I knew I'd have to be more careful.

Then it was time for drawing, and I tried to show the kids how to make a cow look like more than a stick figure. They all held up their drawings and told the group what they drew. One boy was drawing his cow with a purple crayon that broke when he put too much pressure on it.

"That doesn't look like a cow," one of the kids observed.

The boy just smiled. "It's really a lamb," he said calmly, as if he had the power to change one thing into another effortlessly. Which, in a way, I guess he did.

Later I passed out song books for the singing of "Row, Row, Row Your Boat." I ambitiously decided to divide our group in half, with one half singing the first verse and the other half singing the second.

This proved to be a mistake. No one could remember what group they were in, and most just forgot the words.

Rita could see how frustrated I looked. "Don't worry, Cathy," she said in a serious tone. "You're learning."

My first impulse was to laugh in her face. As if I had anything to learn! As if I was the one who couldn't remember which group of three kids I was in! But then something made me stop and think about what she was saying. Maybe there was something that I could learn from her. But was I really learning it?

Suddenly, the head counselor reappeared. Maybe it was my momentarily puzzled look, or maybe it was the fact that we were all just sitting there doing nothing. But once again she said that we should talk in private.

"Listen, Cathy," she said, "there aren't that many days of camp, and we need to make the most of every minute. If things don't go smoothly the first time, there's not a lot of opportunity to make up for it. Maybe this just isn't the right job for you."

Oh God! Now she was going to fire me! I wouldn't even make it through the first day! Needless to say, my parents definitely wouldn't want to send me to gymnastics camp. And what would they think of me?

Just then I heard Rita's voice off to the side. "We like our teacher," she said emphatically. "Don't we, everyone?"

"Yes!" came the answer from the other five kids. "We really like her, and we don't want her to go away!"

It may have been the prospect of having to deal with five angry and disappointed kids, but for whatever reason, the head of the camp abruptly backed off. "Just try to do your best, Cathy," she said with a little smile, and she disappeared as quickly as she had arrived.

At the end of that week, the entire camp got together for a "recital," and my kids sang "Row, Row, Row Your Boat" perfectly. That was amazing, considering what they had been like on the first day. But something else was even more remarkable. As I listened to them sing the song, the thought of gymnastics camp never once crossed my mind. Not for a second.

As it turned out, I did go to the camp that summer, and my Olympic dream is still alive. But when I imagine winning the gold medal these days, I don't think of my picture on television or on the front of a cereal box. I think of my sister, who I hope will be proud of me, hitting her little fists together and laughing with joy.

—w—

Malchut Summary

According to Kabbalistic teachings, our world is the lowest level of reality. What's more, "our world" refers not only to the planet Earth but to the entire created universe, from the most distant galaxies to the tiniest subatomic particles. All of this is the dimension known as *Malchut* in Hebrew, or Kingdom in English.

Does it seem strange that the lowest level of being is referred to as a Kingdom? You might expect a name that would sound a bit less noble. But Malchut is not inferior to the other Sefirot. It is only "low" in the sense that the energy of the Creator is less direct here than in the realms above us. In fact, if that spiritual energy were not indirect, the vast majority of human beings would not be able to exist. The divine power would be too strong for the people who were trying to receive it—as if jet engine fuel were put in the tank of an ordinary automobile. The car would not run, and there might even be an explosion. As we develop our soul's full potential, however, our consciousness becomes able to climb through higher and higher dimensions of spiritual energy. In fact, enabling ourselves to make that climb is the fundamental purpose of our lives.

Does this seem a bit too philosophical? After all, you may not spend much time thinking about your "fundamental purpose."

You're too busy dealing with hundreds of other concerns. And those concerns can seem very important, even if they're less spiritually significant.

But that's just the point! They aren't less spiritually significant. Just as a full-grown tree is concealed within a tiny seed, every action and every moment of your life is an opportunity for connection with immense spiritual power. Indeed, there is literally no limit to what this power can do. It can even grant you eternal life. The only limits to this power are set by your capacity to receive it. It's as if an exciting and informative book were sitting on a shelf in your home—but if you don't know how to read, even the greatest book will never be able to help you.

There's no reason why a life-changing book has to be a thousand pages long. Even reading a short poem can be an unforgettable experience. Kabbalah doesn't make a sharp distinction between what's big and what's small in life. Instead, Kabbalah shows how *all* our experiences are valuable. They can all give us a chance to take responsibility and to reject the temptation to shift this responsibility to anyone else. Does that sound like fun? Maybe not at first—but it's one absolute necessity for having the life you really want.

In the story you've just read, Cathy, for example, is totally focused on her gymnastics camp, to the extent that everything else seems unimportant. All she cares about is becoming an Olympic medal winner—and since winning a medal is something that she can do only alone, all her attention is directed toward herself and her own needs.

Cathy's parents have to look at a wider range of issues. They have to think not only of what's best for Cathy but also of what's best for the needs of their other daughter. And no matter what happens, they are going to have to pay for all of it.

Early in the story, from her completely self-centered perspective, Cathy understands none of this. But by the end, her point of view has shifted. She no longer sees her interests as higher than, or even separate from, those of her sister Rita. What used to be only about her is now about both of them. What used to be two things is now one. Cathy still thinks about winning a gold medal, but now she sees it as an experience that she and Rita will share together.

The tale of Jacob and Rachel deals with similar themes, but in greater detail. The story describes two families. Jacob's family includes his father, Isaac; his mother, Rebecca; and his very aggressive and somewhat brutal brother, Esau. Rachel's family consists of Laban, her father; Rebecca, her mother; and Leah, her older sister. Both these families have their share of secrets and deceptions, as do many families today. The parents have hopes and dreams for their children, and the children have ideas of their own. And again like modern families, sometimes the children's plans are in synch with those of their parents and sometimes they're very far from it. In an amazing way, however, events take place that reveal both the strengths and weaknesses of the two families—and Jacob, for one, comes out better and wiser than he went in. But it wasn't easy!

Like Cathy with her gymnastics, Jacob knows what he wants and is determined to get it. He wants Rachel for his wife, and her beauty blinds him to other things that are going on. We might think, for example, that Jacob would have learned something from the trick that he and his mother played on Isaac. He might have learned to be very suspicious of people who seemed to want to give him something, when what they really wanted was to take something for themselves.

What, for example, does Laban want? Like Cathy's parents, he has to deal with finances as well as emotions. He probably wants someone to help him with his work as a herdsman and farmer. He seems eager enough to sign Jacob on for seven years of labor in exchange for Rachel's hand in marriage. But Laban sees how deeply Jacob loves Rachel. He suspects (correctly) that if Jacob is willing to work seven years in order to marry Rachel, maybe he'll also work fourteen years. Laban hides his plan behind the custom of marrying off the older daughter first, but what he really wants is a free worker. Though the story takes place in ancient times, Laban is a businessman, and in Jacob he sees a way to get something for nothing and to marry off his daughters at the same time.

Perhaps Laban also enlisted Rachel in his plan. She certainly seems to have things very well figured out, what with her "secret word" that was not as secret as Jacob had thought. She might really have felt sorry for her sister—and, like her father, Rachel might have sensed that Jacob would do anything for her, if she just batted her eyelashes hard enough.

Because of all the factors influencing the other people in their lives, both Cathy and Jacob have to do something that they really don't want to do. Cathy has to work at her sister's day camp, and Jacob has to marry Leah. True, it's infuriating when other people's agendas get in the way of our own plans, but that's what happens sometimes. In fact, it happens many times. It's the very nature of the material world in which we live—of Malchut, where all the energies of the universe, both positive and negative, create a maze of conflicting wants and needs. Our challenge is to find our way through that maze. In fact, if we hope to get what we want, we have no choice. We have to do some things that really turn us off if we want to do the things that really turn us on.

But here's the surprising part—so surprising, in fact, that very few people believe it until it actually happens to them. If you perform the task that seems so absolutely repulsive to you, not only will you get what you wanted, but you'll get much more than you wanted. You'll change and grow in ways you never imagined. But you can't know that until you've gotten through the challenge that seemed so overwhelming.

The two stories you've read deal with situations that may be different from your own experiences, but these same factors are at work every day of your life. Whether you like it or not, the world is

32

set up in such a way that obstacles will appear between you and your desires. This happens in every area of life—big and small, major and minor, short term and long term. Whether it's about the school you want to attend or who gets to use the television remote, things in this world don't fall into place automatically. Sometimes (many times!) you're the one who'll have to change and adjust. Once it's all over, you'll be glad you did—but as we've said, it's always hard to know that going in.

Of course, there is another choice. You can always attempt to take yourself out of the game. You can say "I quit" and try to withdraw from the situation entirely. But the word *try* should be emphasized here, because according to Kabbalisitc teachings, you can never really decide simply to avoid the challenges that come up in your life. The reason for this is very clear: it is your destiny to overcome those challenges and to become a completely joyful and fulfilled person. If you choose not to deal with them now, the same issues will keep reappearing until you finally take care of them once and for all. This process can happen quickly, or it can happen slowly. You can do the work now, or you can stretch it out over many years or even over many lifetimes. However, quitting is not an option, however tempting it may appear.

When Cathy's parents told her she would have to work at Rita's day camp in order to go to Minnesota to practice gymnastics, she could have said, "I don't care about gymnastics! I'm going into my room to listen to my Walkman!" When Jacob found out that he couldn't marry the woman he loved unless he first married the woman he didn't love, he could have backed out. He could have said, "Rachel is great, but there are a lot of other fish in the sea. I'll find somebody else." Or he could have taken "the high road." He could have refused on principle to marry Leah, even though it would have meant losing Rachel forever.

Often people will choose to forego something they really want because it also requires something they don't want. But Kabbalah teaches that this is usually a big mistake. As the ancient Kabbalists put it: "We should love Leah as we love Rachel." We should love the difficulties as much as we love the rewards.

In fact, we should love the difficulties more than we love the rewards. If there had been no obstacles, you would have gotten what you desired. By overcoming obstacles—both within yourself and in the outside world—not only will you *receive* more than you expected, but you will also become what you are really supposed to be and that is a stronger, wiser, and happier person than you started out. The people in our two stories found this out, and you can make the same discovery.

CHAPTER TWO

Ysod

The Bridge Between Worlds

Ysod filters the energies of the upper Sefirot so they can reveal themselves in the physical world. True, we can and should become capable of accessing the higher levels more directly, but this is the work of a lifetime. For now, we should learn to connect with these energies in their "safe" form, after they have crossed the bridge of Ysod.

As you become aware of the unlimited spiritual potential within you, it's important to be aware that sometimes "too much of a good thing" may not work for you. This applies to spirituality as well as to everything else in life, especially in our society. At the dinner table, we don't just eat until we're satisfied; we eat until all the food is gone. Similarly, the lines to buy lottery tickets get longer when the payoff becomes truly astronomical—because there's no such thing as too much money, right? "Too much" is not a concept that comes naturally to us. Of course, God is aware of our human tendency to go overboard, and the Sefirah of Ysod exists to deal with that tendency. To explain this, we can use the high-tech metaphor Through Ysod, the love, wisdom, and power of the Creator are downloaded into the world in a form that we, like human computers, can use and understand.

Sometimes people look for shortcuts to spirituality. They want the secrets of the universe, and they want them now. Trances, drugs, and even walks across hot coals can certainly be very intense experiences, but they can't bring wisdom to anyone who really isn't ready to receive it. And if a person is ready to receive the Light of God, there's no need for shortcuts in the first place. As someone once said, "When the student is ready, the teacher will appear."

—⟋⟋⟍—

Ysod ensures that you will connect with God in the way that's best for you right now—nothing more, and certainly nothing less. Sometimes other people may have a stronger connection right now, based on how far their souls have traveled on the journey to God. There's much to be learned from just being in the presence of such people, even if the lessons are not always easy to understand.

The Baal Shem Tov

The great Kabbalist known as the Baal Shem Tov—that is, "The Master of the Holy Name"—lived in Eastern Europe during the eighteenth century, a time of intense interest in the mystical aspects of the Jewish religion. Once, this great spiritual master arrived unexpectedly in a small town. It was a Friday evening, just as the Sabbath was about to begin. As the service proceeded, all the people of the town were excited and honored by the presence of a true holy person (in Hebrew called a *tzaddik*), who for some unknown reason had decided to visit them. Naturally, they hoped that he would join them in their homes after the service ended—but to their great disappointment, he declined every invitation.

In fact, the Baal Shem Tov chose not to leave the synagogue at all. He remained just where he was after the service ended, and as he began to pray, the townspeople were amazed and even a bit frightened by the fervor of his prayer. But even more remarkable was the way the tzaddik continued to pray throughout the entire night.

Although they sensed that something must have been terribly wrong to require such praying, the townspeople had no idea what the problem was.

The next morning, however, the Baal Shem Tov was perfectly relaxed and joyful. Although he had not slept a wink, he seemed energized and joyful. And when one of the townspeople offered him an invitation to the morning Sabbath meal, the tzaddik gladly accepted.

Of course, all the townspeople crowded into the house of the host to see the great sage. Just then, as everyone was seated around the table, a local peasant burst into the house and asked for a drink of vodka. The townspeople were about to drive him away, but the Baal Shem Tov called out that he should be brought into the dining room and be provided with a generous glass of vodka. This was done, and as the peasant enjoyed his drink, the Baal Shem Tov asked him whether anything unusual had taken place during the previous evening.

With his tongue loosened by the vodka, the peasant declared that something very unusual indeed had occurred. It seemed that the local nobleman and landlord, believing that a Jewish merchant had cheated him in a business deal, assembled his peasants and armed them with knives and hatchets. He was going to incite them to attack and kill all the Jews for miles around. In this way, he promised them, they would be able to liberate all the riches that the Jews had supposedly stolen. The nobleman was even planning to let the peasants keep some of the supposedly stolen riches, though most of it would, of course, be turned over to him.

"The whole night we waited for the command to attack," the peasant continued. "But then the nobleman closeted himself in his chamber with an unexpected visitor—an old friend that he hadn't seen for forty years. Finally he emerged and told us all to go home because he had made a big mistake. He now realized that the Jews were upright and honest people and nobody should dare lay a hand on them. So we all went home. We were disappointed, but there's no way to understand what goes through the mind of these nobles. The best thing to do is just stay drunk all the time, as I'm doing now."

This incident involving the Baal Shem Tov became very well known throughout the region, though most people had a great deal of trouble understanding it. Somehow, to be sure, the tzaddik's fervent prayer had been responsible for the salvation of the town's Jews, but no one was sure exactly how this had been accomplished. Finally, the Baal Shem Tov himself explained the mystery. "You see," he declared, "the friend that the nobleman had not seen in forty years had actually been dead that entire time. By the power of prayer, I was able to drag him from the grave in order to prevent the murderous attack."

While this was obviously the correct explanation, one of the townspeople asked a question that was in many people's minds. "Why," he inquired, "did you have to travel all the way to our town for Sabbath to avert the attack? Couldn't you have just as well remained in his hometown of Medzibuz and sent forth your prayers from there?"

The Baal Shem Tov just smiled. "If I succeeded in saving your town, that would have been a great gift," he said. "But if I failed and there had been an attack, then at least I would have been able to die along with you."

—⚶—

Sometimes we find ourselves puzzled by life. Then we think we've understood, only to find ourselves puzzled again. What's the lesson? That understanding is a journey, not a destination.

Cassandra

Nick was having one of those days. Nothing went right. He didn't just fall off his bike and dent it, but he also ripped his new Dockers and sprained his wrist. On top of that, he wasn't doing so well in school, and today was the first day his tutor was coming over. Now, he couldn't even hold a pencil in his hand! What kind of world was this? So he just sulked around the house.

"Nick, why don't you go to the street fair?" his father asked.

"Because I can't ride my bike there!"

"Well, you can walk. What's the hurry? Stop rushing your life away. It'll go by fast enough—believe me."

For the millionth time, Nick wondered why his parents always talked about how old they were. And he also wondered why they couldn't just leave him alone.

But he did end up walking to the street fair. It took forever—and he would have been there in five minutes with his bike. Still, there were some interesting things: vinyl records from the days of the dinosaurs, a blues band playing, and booths with stuff you might not exactly want to eat, but that did smell good.

Nick stopped at a booth selling used books. There before his eyes was a copy of *Cassandra, the Warrior*. Last summer, when that book had been on his assigned reading list, Nick had felt no interest in reading it. Like the vinyl records, it seemed like something connected to ancient history—the Greeks, maybe—and Nick had enough problems right here in the modern world. But when he actually looked into the book, he really liked it.

"Are you reading *Cassandra, the Warrior*?"

Nick turned in the direction of the voice he'd heard. For a split second he was startled; there was no one there! Then he looked down and saw a young woman somewhat older than himself, in her mid-twenties, probably. She was in a wheelchair.

"I read it last summer," Nick told the woman. "Cassandra was really brave. I mean, how she survived everything that happened to her." Nick hesitated. He felt uncomfortable telling a disabled woman about the story of a disabled girl.

"You read it too?" he finally asked.

"Well, it was written about me," she said. "I'm Carrie, but I'm Cassandra in the book." She laughed. "I can prove it. Ask me anything!"

I did. I asked her if when she survived the car accident, had she really become stronger or weaker.

"I can't do as much physically, of course. But mentally, I can land on Mars, and survive. I'd find my way around anywhere, and I'd do very well. I take better care of myself too. I've learned not to rush life. Also, I don't drive so fast, for one thing. There are miracles out there, but we don't slow down enough to see them."

Nick didn't know exactly how to respond to this. "I'd like to shake your hand," he said, "but I sprained my wrist really bad in a bicycle accident." But Nick quickly realized this was the wrong thing to say. Looking down, he saw that Carrie had lost her right arm.

"I'm really sorry," he said softly.

"Hey, I'm lucky. It was a miracle."

"But—"

"There's so much you don't know," she interrupted. "Sometimes I think it was meant to be. I met my husband because of the accident. First he was my neurosurgeon, and now he's my soul mate. It's how things were supposed to happen. Or at least that's how I've decided to look at it."

"Well, I've already read this book, but I'd like to have another copy," Nick said. A sticker on the cover indicated a price of fifty cents. It seemed insultingly low. On the other hand, what price would really have seemed high enough?

"Will you sign it for me?" Nick asked—another mistake, but somehow he was now able to laugh about it. "I mean, can you sign it with your left hand?"

"Sure!"

Nick handed her the book, and with a practiced one-handed motion, Carrie opened her purse and took out a pen. She wrote something in the book, then smiled and handed it back to Nick. Their moment together was over. Carrie pushed a button on the controls of her chair, and with a soft whirring sound, she glided away.

You know, if I survived an accident, I might think it was a miracle, but it was probably just good luck. It could have gone the other way. She could have kept the arm—but maybe lost her life. Anything could have happened. Why is she so certain it was meant to be? How did she figure that one out? If I didn't sprain my arm, I would be on my bike and wouldn't have met Carrie. But this soul mate business. I wonder if there is such a thing or just two people who are gushy over each other.

Nick left the street fair. He felt energized, felt like running, but he was too old now to run along the sidewalk, unless he was dressed for it. Running now wouldn't look right, so he walked. He held the book in his left hand, the one whose wrist didn't hurt. He still hadn't looked at what she wrote.

All the way home, Nick thought about what she had said. Was it worth losing your ability to walk in order to find someone you loved? Was it worth your right arm to find somebody who loved you? Was any of that really miraculous?

At home, Nick found his mother in the living room reading one of the long novels she called page-turners. It was amazing how fast she could read them. It seemed strange to him that she wanted to read so many books. On the other hand, he knew that television and video games seemed strange from her point of view. He was feeling calmer now for some reason. He felt like philosophizing about that kind of stuff.

"How was the street fair?" she asked, without looking up.

"Mom," he said, "the most amazing thing happened."

She caught the urgent note in his voice. She looked up now. "It did?"

"Definitely." He held up the book. "I met the woman that this book is about. She was at the street fair. It was an amazing coincidence. And that was only part of it."

Nick's mother nodded. She looked interested. "What else, dear?"

"Well, you know how I hurt my arm?" he said. "She hurt her arm too. I mean, she actually *lost* her arm."

"That's amazing."

"Yeah, it really was."

She smiled and looked back at her page-turner. Sometimes Nick got angry when she didn't want to talk with him. Since he usually didn't want to talk, shouldn't she pay attention whenever he finally did? But he wasn't angry now. He loved her. He was still feeling philosophical, but now with love added to it. His wrist no longer hurt. The day had started out badly, but now it had become so good.

Nick went into the kitchen. He sat down at the table. There was still one thing he had to do. He wanted to do it, but he also didn't want to. He didn't want to lose the feeling of having it in him. But he also really, really wanted to see what Carrie had written in the book.

Nick opened it to the title page. There were just two lines of her writing. Nick read: "I'm not the girl in this book. But it's still a miracle that we met."

Nick closed the book. He could feel the calm and peace that had enveloped him at the street fair starting to strain and approach the breaking point, like a stretched rubber band. Stretching and stretching—but for some reason it didn't break. He could see that the woman—whoever she was—had been right after all. It was a miracle that they'd met. It was a miracle that they'd read the same book, that they were living at the same time, in the same city, at the same street fair. Nick knew that someday he would meet the real Cassandra from the book. It was even better this way. It was better to have it before him.

—〰—

Ysod Summary

Although it may appear that we all inhabit the same reality, how can we be sure of this? How can you know that the color blue looks the same to you as it does to the person standing next to you? On a deeper level, can you be certain that you experience feelings like sadness or joy in the same way that other people feel them? The truth is, we can't really know what anyone else experiences, either physically or emotionally—and most of the time, we don't have to know. In the everyday world, we can get along by not looking too closely at the basic difficulty of getting inside someone else's skin.

Kabbalah teaches that certain people are gifted with much higher levels of perception than others are. The Baal Shem Tov, for example, could see into the future and the past. Nick, in the preceding story, wanted to connect with that higher level of perception. He wanted to take part in a mystical experience of life. He wanted to believe that a miraculous coincidence had taken place in his meeting the real-life heroine of his book. As it turned out, that was not quite what happened. But Nick gained an insight into an even higher level of understanding. No matter what happens in your life, the opportunity to see a miracle is always there. But you need to recognize that opportunity and take advantage of it.

Great sages—*tzaddikim*—such as the Baal Shem Tov, are people who have reached the highest levels of awareness and sensitivity. Kabbalah teaches that they have earned the right to live in paradise, but they have returned to this world because they want to help others. This return represents a great sacrifice on the part of the tzaddikim. It certainly would be much easier to remain in the Upper World, where the pain and suffering of life on earth have been left far behind. It is said that at any given moment there are 72 tzaddikim living in the world; 36 of them are revealed and recognized as great souls, while the other 36 remain hidden.

During the early part of his life the Baal Shem Tov was one of the hidden tzaddikim, but later he was recognized and admired for his supreme spiritual power. He prayed with such intensity that he seemed to be speaking directly to God. Yet even those who knew him were often mystified by his sometimes unpredictable and

Who Is a Tzaddik?

Sometimes tzaddikim are easy to recognize, and sometimes identifying them is very difficult. There are certain people, for example, whose goodness is obvious to everyone. They are universally loved and respected. Other tzaddikim, however, choose to remain hidden. They may even disguise themselves as negative or evil people in order to prevent their revelation; they do their good work in secret. These hidden tzaddikim resist coming out into the open. They have no wish to be honored and admired. They only make themselves known during times of crisis, when there is desperate need for their help.

unnerving behavior—like suddenly praying for an extended period. Being close to the Baal Shem Tov was a huge honor and opportunity, but it also presented many challenges. When the Master did something that seemed to make no sense—his followers simply had to trust that there was something going on that they were not empowered to see but that would turn out well in the end.

This is exactly what's needed in our relationship with God. Often, maybe most of the time, it may seem that things are happening in ways that make no sense at all. Or if they do make sense, it's in a very unpleasant and dangerous way. It may seem like "the world is against you," which is how Nick felt at the beginning of the story preceding. What we need to remember is this: events may not happen the way we want them to, and often there's nothing we can do about that. The causes are simply beyond our control. On the other hand, our responses to events are always within our control. This is a great opportunity and also a great responsibility. It means that no matter what takes place, we've the option to react negatively or positively. We've the freedom to choose trust or despair. Of course, making the best choice is not easy. It isn't supposed to be easy, because growth is rarely easy or without discomfort. But by making use of difficulties instead of just reacting to them, we can move closer to the joy and fulfillment that is our true destiny.

Kabbalah teaches that the reality we inhabit is the one we need to inhabit. The unique world in which each of us lives provides the maximum connection with God that we can handle, and some people can handle more than others can. The Baal Shem Tov is more directly connected to God than a boy who feels victimized because he sprained his wrist.

Conventional religion often gives the impression that we should ask God for more. Kabbalah, however, advises us to *be* more in our own right—not be more like anyone else, but be more aware of the miracles that are always going on around us. This is what our spiritual capacity enlarges, and what we receive from God will grow as well. The Sefirah of Ysod exists to maintain that balance. It is the energy regulator of the spiritual system. As you grow, the energy you receive grows proportionally.

Surprisingly, it's not always easy to realize, or to accept, that growth is taking place. Nick had a spiritual experience, even if it's not the one he thought he had. There's a lesson here: don't fail to recognize positive changes that are taking place, even if they're not the ones you expected and even if you have to look for them.

The Tycher Library
in the
Mankoff Center for Jewish Learning

CHAPTER THREE

Hod

Purpose and Persistence

od is the power to *move forward*. It's the energy that allows you to move closer to all your life's goals—both the short-term objectives, such as doing well in school or choosing a career, and the ultimate purpose of creating unity with God in your heart and soul.

The Sefirah of Hod and Netzach, the one that comes after it, are often described as two closely related parts of a single whole. They're like the arms or legs of the human body. They're separate, but they generally work together. Netzach is associated with the idea of victory—the overcoming of inner and outer obstacles. Hod is the emotion that accompanies that victory. It's the experience of something beautiful and awe inspiring. When you've worked hard to accomplish a specific task and you finally get it done, there's often a moment of disbelief: "Did I really do that?"

We've all seen television images of athletes at the moment of winning an important contest. They fall to their knees on the tennis court or the soccer field. At least for a second or two, the look on their faces is not really happiness, but amazement. This is just a glimpse of the energy of Hod, although the Kabbalists would remind us that even winning the Olympics can't be compared with coming into the presence of God.

As with all the Sefirot, Hod encompasses not only our own experience but also our power to inspire that experience in others. Moses, for example, caused people to feel awestruck in his presence. The Kabbalists tell us that he was more than just a great leader. He was a person who had literally stood in the presence of God, and God's power and love shone through Moses' being.

Just as Moses led his people through the desert for forty years, Hod is the energy that helps our souls to move forward through each day, each year, and over each lifetime. It's the determination we feel when we're in the presence of a truly powerful being. As such, we should always feel connected to the Sefirah of Hod, since we are always in the presence of God.

The following story concerns a key teaching of the Sefirah of Hod: what seems like a fall is really a step upward.

The Clown

Most of the nobility who ruled Poland in the eighteenth and nineteenth centuries had no interest in anything besides enriching themselves through the labor of their impoverished peasantry. But from time to time a nobleman would appear who wished to modernize the lands under his ownership. Once, a modernizer of this kind decided that he wanted to build a road through an old Jewish cemetery. The members of the local burial society, therefore, were ordered to unearth all the remains of all the deceased and move them to a new location.

Traditional Jewish law forbids the use of elaborate metal caskets. In fact, the simple wooden caskets in which Jews were buried over the centuries seemed designed to decompose as quickly as possible. There were several reasons for this. For one thing, the spirit of the deceased was understood to remain with the body for a period of three days after death. The flimsy casket was intended to make the spirit's departure as easy as possible when the time finally arrived. Furthermore, when the wooden casket decomposed, the body would have an easier time reuniting with the surrounding earth, as it is written, "Dust thou art, and to dust thou shalt return."

Indeed, when the bodies were exhumed virtually all of them were found to have decomposed. Only flimsy skeletons remained. But there was one astonishing exception. To their amazement, the members of the burial society found one body that had not decomposed at all. On the rare occasions that this occurs, it is a sign that the deceased had been a person of great righteousness. But in this case there was something even more astonishing. The perfectly preserved body had been buried in the costume of a clown!

The name on the tombstone of this mysterious individual was Rabbi Naftali. Inquiries were made among the elders of the town, and one very old man did in fact recall the story of Rabbi Naftali, though the actual events had taken place long, long ago. With some encouragement, the old man's memories became more vivid, and this is the story that emerged.

What Is a Rabbi?

The word *rabbi* derives from a Hebrew root meaning "teacher." Originally, it was an honorary term given to a respected member of a community who, by virtue of extraordinary learning and good character, was qualified to teach the lessons of the Bible and to make rulings on the applications of Jewish law in daily life. More recently, especially in America, rabbi has become a title granted by recognized academic or theological institutions, just as the title "doctor" is conferred by medical schools.

It seemed that Rabbi Naftali had occupied the position of *Gabbai Tzedakah*, or "charity helper." The responsibilities of this position were quite clear, but were by no means easy. He had to make sure that everyone in the town contributed as much as possible to support those who were in need of help. This went on throughout the year, but from time to time emergencies would also arise. When this happened, it fell to the Gabbai Tzedakah to raise the necessary funds and to deal with whatever the circumstances happened to be.

On one occasion, the responsibilities of a Gabbai Tzedakah seemed to fall especially heavily on Rabbi Naftali. He had just finished collecting the regular contributions from the townspeople when a man knocked on his door. "Please, you must help me!" the man begged. "I have nowhere else to turn!"

Already burdened by the expenses of a large family, one of the man's children had suddenly fallen ill, and there was no money to pay for a doctor. Without hesitation, Rabbi Naftali went out to collect once again. Fortunately, the townspeople were able to help, though their contributions were smaller than they might have been because the regular donations had just been made. Although he realized that everyone was facing difficulties of their own and that no one was rich, Rabbi Naftali was very persuasive in communicating the problems of the man with the sick child. Finally, he returned home exhausted but satisfied that he had done the right thing. The distraught father was overjoyed to receive the money, and the life of his child would now be saved.

But just as Rabbi Naftali was lying down to rest, there was another knock on his door. This time it was a man with a house whose roof had caved in. He had ten children, and now they were all homeless. It seemed almost impossible that Naftali could go around collecting three times in one day—but he did. It was impossible, however, to expect that the already impoverished townspeople could contribute any more money, even in so desperate a cause. Rabbi Naftali, therefore, was forced to approach the young son of the local nobleman, who was entertaining some of his friends at a nearby pub. Rabbi Naftali did this without much hope of success, however, since it was well known that those who had the most money were the least likely to share it with anyone in need.

As Rabbi Naftali described the problem of the man who had lost his home, the young nobleman laughed and shouted out loud. "That's what people get for living in poorly constructed dwellings. If he had any brains, he'd live in a castle like me. Or, should I say, he'd live in a castle if he had any money! Ha ha!" Then he and his friends all began to ridicule Rabbi Naftali mercilessly. But all of a sudden, the young man had an idea.

"Rabbi Naftali," he exclaimed, "how would you like to have the entire amount of money you need? We will give it to you on one condition. All you have to do is to walk through the main street of town wearing the costume of a clown!"

Rabbi Naftali immediately agreed. He was not eager to be humiliated, but his personal dignity meant nothing compared to the welfare of the people who were depending on him. So he dressed in a clown suit and walked down the main street of the town, with the young nobles following behind him singing, laughing, and occasionally throwing things at him whenever they felt the urge. But true to their word, they did give him the money, which Rabbi Naftali immediately passed on to the homeless man, who would now be able to get a room in an inn for his family.

As for Rabbi Naftali, he went home a broken man. He threw the clown suit in the back of his closet and collapsed onto bed. His only hope was that no other needy people would come to his door that day and that he could at last get some rest.

A year later, it so happened that the great tzaddik Rabbi Chaim of Tzanz was traveling through that same town. Just as he was passing the home of Rabbi Naftali, he abruptly stopped and exclaimed, "I hear beautiful music coming from that house! It is the music of the Garden of Eden!" Hearing these words, the followers of Rabbi

Chaim knocked on Rabbi Naftali's door and began to question him. What had he ever done that would cause the music of Eden to emanate from his house?

Rabbi Naftali had no idea how to answer their questions. He certainly did not think of himself as an estimable person in any sense. In fact, he admitted that he had lost all respect for himself since the incident of the clown suit.

"The clown suit?" Rabbi Chaim inquired. "Can you tell me what that incident entailed?" Reluctantly, Rabbi Naftali explained how the young noblemen had humiliated him in order to raise money for charity. He even showed Rabbi Chaim the clown suit that had lain in his closet ever since.

At the sight of the clown suit, Rabbi Chaim commanded the members of the local burial society that when Rabbi Naftali's time came, he should be buried in this same regalia. The angels of destruction, who are responsible for the dissolution of people's physical bodies after death, would not dare to touch him.

—ᘛᘚ—

To get what you need, sometimes you must lose what you have. To see what's really important, sometimes you have to look beyond the things that have dominated your point of view. The boy in the following story is used to getting back on his feet after being knocked down— but now he's called on to do that, not just in a physical sense, but spiritually as well.

Football, Lacrosse, . . . and Beyond

Even when I was very young, I never had a problem getting back on my feet after getting knocked down—and I was knocked down a lot! When my two older brothers and the other kids in the neighborhood played football in the park, I was always the smallest player on the field. But I didn't really mind. In fact, I liked the challenge of succeeding at things that no one expected me to accomplish. When I tackled a bigger kid, my height may have remained under five feet, but I felt as tall as the treetops.

Football was the sport that received the most attention in our family, and we played it even during the summer. We'd take just a short break to watch the World Series. In fact, for a number of years I actually believed that football was the only sport or, at least, the only one worth playing. I used to daydream about being a star in high school and college. Sometimes I'd really let my imagination run free and picture myself as a player on a professional team. Could that really happen? Well, I certainly did everything I could in that direction, from lifting lots of weights to eating plenty of Wheaties.

As time went by, however, reality did begin to set in. My brothers were on the football team at our high school, but neither of them became stars. For me, this wasn't a good sign at all, since both of them were bigger and stronger than I was. And it didn't look like things were going to change very much. It's not that I didn't grow, but I just seemed to grow more slowly than most people did.

When it was my turn to enter ninth grade, my brothers sat me down for a serious talk. They asked me if I was planning to try out for the football team. I looked at them as if they'd just asked me whether I intended to keep breathing. I laughed. "Of course I'm planning to try out!"

I was a little surprised that they didn't laugh with me, or even at me. I was used to being challenged in that way by them, and it just made me try harder. But this was very different. They seemed so serious.

By the time we were finished with that discussion, I had been thoroughly discouraged from playing high school football. Most remarkably, this hadn't involved teasing or laughing at me. It was sincere concern for my physical and emotional well-being. My brothers were concerned that I would get hurt and humiliated. In a way, it was a real turning point in our relationship. I couldn't recall their ever talking to me that way before. It was something of a pleasant surprise.

But surprise wasn't the strongest feeling that came out of that conversation, however. My most intense emotion by far was disappointment. I had devoted so much time to planning and preparing for my football career that I could hardly imagine my future without it. But I knew that my brothers were being straight with me. For maybe the first time, I knew that they really had my best interests at heart. Most difficult of all, I knew they were right.

By the time I entered high school, I had resigned myself to concentrating on my studies and forgetting about my dreams of athletic glory. Things went this way for the first several months. Then, just as spring was beginning, something happened that would really change my life. As I was leaving school one afternoon, I saw some kids on their way to the athletic field carrying helmets and what looked like long-handled sticks with webbed baskets on one end. Somehow I knew they were lacrosse players, although I don't think that I had ever actually seen lacrosse players in the flesh. But one thing caught my attention right away: *they weren't very big*. They were certainly a lot smaller than the school's football players were. In fact, most of them were just my size!

Twenty-four hours later, I was among the lacrosse players heading out to practice. Since I had never used one of those strange sticks before, catching and throwing the hard rubber ball was a real comedy of errors, especially while trying to see through the elaborate face guard on the helmet. But it was the kind of challenge I enjoyed, and I could tell right away that I had some talent for it.

Soon I was using every free moment to practice lacrosse. I carried the stick everywhere, learning to shift the ball back and forth in the webbing as I ran. As an extra added attraction, my brothers were very inept at this game. When I let them try to catch the ball, they were much more likely to be hit in the head than to use the stick effectively. Overall, lacrosse was great. I had found a new identity as an athlete, and very soon that became my identity as a person too.

For the next three years, I got better and better at lacrosse. During the competitive season, of course, I was totally obsessed, and throughout the rest of the year I practiced as much as I could. I attended special lacrosse camps during the summers, and I read every book on lacrosse that I could possibly find. It was exciting to be part of a sport that was quickly gaining in popularity. Just as I had once focused on playing football in high school, I now devoted myself to preparing for the experience of playing lacrosse in college. I followed the results of the annual national championship tournaments, and during the summer before my junior year I started writing e-mail inquiries to the coaches at the various schools. All this was really exciting. Even my parents were excited, since most of the major lacrosse schools were also in the top rank academically. If I was going to get into Princeton or Johns Hopkins, I would have to study as well as play my favorite game. So that is exactly what I did.

The late summer before starting twelfth grade, I was invited to play on our state all-star team at a national lacrosse tournament in California. This was a real honor, but it didn't really surprise me. In fact, it was pretty much expected that anyone who wanted to play major college lacrosse would play in this tournament. All the college coaches would be there to watch. Players who did well could expect to be offered full scholarships. Players who did less than well, on the other hand, couldn't expect to receive much attention.

As it turned out, I was playing really well. On the second day of the tournament, however, I sustained a very severe injury to ligaments in my right knee. It was a very common injury, but also it was one that required surgery and a long recovery period. The outcome of all this was very hard to predict. Sometimes there were no long-term effects, and for other people, there was a real falloff in their ability to play the game. One thing was for sure. The college coaches who had come to watch the tournament were a lot less interested in me after they saw me taken off the field.

Of course, I felt completely destroyed by this. It was like re-living my disappointment about playing high school football, but this was a hundred times worse. I had completely morphed into being a lacrosse player, and now that was all being called into question. It was like waking up one morning and discovering that you are not the person you thought you were—but without any idea of whom you had turned into.

There was also the rather scary experience of having surgery on my knee. It happened very quickly. As soon as I got home from California, a doctor examined me, and I was immediately admitted to a hospital. The idea was to get the rehabilitation process started very quickly so that I could tell the colleges as soon as possible that I was completely healed. Now, by the way, my brothers and my parents were at least as into my athletic career as I was. I had become the sports star. Without a doubt, that was exactly what I had always wanted to be, but now the actual experience of it was changing fast. Since the injury, being the star was more like a responsibility than a pleasure. Suddenly it seemed like this was something I was doing for other people instead of for myself; it was less like playing the lead role in an action movie and more like some chore—taking out the garbage, for instance.

On the morning of my operation, I was brought to the "pre-op room" on a gurney and was left in a small space with curtains separating me from other patients awaiting surgery. But before I was wheeled into my cubicle, I could see that the space next to me was occupied by a girl about my age who seemed to have suffered some sort of severe neck injury. I could see that her head was being supported by a metal framework that looked like a halo around her head. It was not a very attractive sight. In fact, it was quite frightening. Her eyes were closed and she looked like she was sleeping. Actually, she was probably under some form of heavy sedation.

While I was waiting in my cubicle, I thought of the girl lying on the other side of the curtain. She was separated from me by a piece of cloth, but there were some other much more important separations between us. We didn't know each other. We didn't care about each other. There was an excellent chance we would never see each other's faces or exchange a single word.

I'm not sure how this happened, but suddenly I realized how artificial those differences really were. It wasn't so much that I had lost touch with the way I felt about myself, but I began to feel—to really experience—what it felt like to be her. Although I thought of myself as a tough athlete, I now understood, or thought I understood, what it was like to be a young girl with a metal halo screwed into her skull and unable even to move. Obviously, her injury was a lot more severe than mine was. But I no longer felt that there was a difference between what was "mine" and what was anybody else's. It was an amazing shift in point of view.

After a few moments I heard some talking from the other side of the curtain, and I realized that the girl's doctor had come in to speak with her about her surgery. As I listened, I found out that she had been in a car accident and had broken her neck. The doctor tried to speak with her as gently as possible, but he had to inform her that there was a risk of paralysis if things did not go as planned during the operation. That was the first time that I heard the girl's voice clearly. She said, "Well, please just try to be really careful." And the doctor said, "We definitely will."

That was the last I heard. My own doctor came into my cubicle and began to speak about the kind of anesthetic that would be used on me. A few minutes later another doctor came in to give me an injection, and that was my last memory until the surgery was over.

I've tried to convey the strange feeling I had that morning in the hospital—the completely unexpected experience of getting outside myself and into the consciousness of another person. If I haven't gotten that across, it's not because it didn't happen. It's just because

I haven't been able to express it. Surprising as this may seem, however, having that feeling isn't really the point of my story because even though it was an amazing experience to have this powerful sensation come on so suddenly, it was even more amazing that it didn't last. For the few moments that I was waiting behind those curtains, although I really was able to get outside myself and feel what someone else was experiencing in life, it didn't last. I wasn't just watching it, like in a movie, but really feeling it. It wasn't like a dream. It was real life. But as convincing as this was, it was gone as soon as I woke up in the recovery room of the hospital, and I was back to the person I had been before, worried about my knee and my athletic career.

There was one way, however, in which the experience was really a lasting one. Before, my main goal in life had been to succeed in sports and to earn a college scholarship. It was all about putting the lacrosse ball in the other team's goal and rejoicing in the results that would come from that. But since my stay in the hospital, I have a new objective. It's to recapture that experience of unity with another human being, or maybe even with all human beings. It's to somehow get outside of myself so that I can really know what other people are thinking and feeling. Somehow, I now believe that everything that happened to me was leading up to that moment in the hospital. Now it's up to me to re-create that moment as often as I can. That's my real objective now, and it isn't made out of metal and rope. It's a spiritual goal, and if it takes a lifetime to achieve it, I'm going to try.

Hod Summary

One of the basic teachings of Kabbalah can be expressed in just five short words: your life has a purpose. There really is a system to the universe, and you have a role to play in it—both for yourself as an individual soul and for you collectively as a part of humanity in general. Even if you never explore this idea any further, the principle that there is a direction to your existence is fundamentally a different perspective from the idea of a random universe that pervades the modern world. And the teachings of Kabbalah go even further, by explaining exactly how the purpose of our lives can be understood and achieved.

The Sefirah of Hod plays a vital role in bringing about that achievement. For example, When the sages of Kabbalah discuss the purpose of human life, they first do so on an individual level. They begin with the proposition that your true destiny is complete happiness and fulfillment. What exactly does that mean? It means, first of all, a sense of having everything you desire—physically, emotionally, and spiritually—and also the intention to *share* that experience with others. It's not enough for you to achieve this level of being. You're determined that others will achieve it also.

In fact, you are destined to life in Paradise forever, just like Adam and Eve before they made their fatal mistake with the serpent. But unlike Adam and Eve, who were created in Paradise, you (and all other human beings) have to earn your way back in. This involves some struggle. It means working on your soul the way a sculptor forms a difficult piece of marble or a gardener tries to cultivate orchids by keeping out the weeds. Each of us, at every moment, has to choose between the path that moves us toward happiness and the path that moves us away from it.

The truth is, most of us choose the wrong path, at least at first. Most of us make the same mistakes repeatedly, so we have to keep coming back for one lifetime after another until we "get it right." What exactly those mistakes might be differ from person to person. Regarding this, the spiritual energy of Hod is extremely important. Hod is associated in the soul with the power to continually advance, with the determination and perseverance born of deep inner commitment toward the realization of one's life goals. The acknowledgment of a supreme purpose in life and of the total submission of self that it inspires serves to endow the source of one's inspiration with an aura of splendor and majesty. For this reason, the Hebrew word *hod* means "splendor" or "scintillation of light."

It's so easy to find reasons why things can't be done. It's always reasonable to stay where you are and avoid the growth pains that come with real change. Whenever you decide to stretch yourself, to extend your limits beyond where they've always been, "rational" thinking will tell you that it's all a big mistake—and the argument is usually extremely convincing. It's as if an inner voice is saying, "What's the use? Don't kid yourself. Be rational. It can never work out."

This kind of thinking lets you accomplish only as much as the negative, self-defeating side of our nature will allow. But a basic purpose of all Kabbalistic teaching is to move us in the other direction, in which we believe not only that we will have a fulfilled life, but that we will have complete *certainty* of it. Abraham the patriarch was a hundred years old when God told him that he would father a son and be the founder of a great nation, and his wife Sarah was in her nineties! Similarly, disaster seemed inevitable when Moses and the Israelites stood on the banks of the Red Sea, with Pharaoh's army rapidly approaching from the rear. But Kabbalah is based on supposed "lost causes," and they turned out to be anything but lost simply because the people in question took action. They trusted in the tools, such as prayer, meditation, and the teachings of Kabbalah, that the Creator had provided for them instead of trusting the very limited evidence of their own perceptions.

When you formulate a goal, remember to think of yourself as a vessel—an open-ended receiver, not closed or limited. If your circumstances seem constricted, recognize the fact that it is your own thoughts and your own desires that are creating this "reality." When you change your consciousness, the situation can change as well. Be aware also that, with any goal, the real objective is a change of con-

sciousness not just the acquisition of a physical object or the participation in a certain event. The Baal Shem Tov was no richer than
anyone else in poverty-stricken Poland in the eighteenth century. Yet
people envied him and wanted to be like him, not for what he *had*,
but for what he was on the inside.

Let's be very clear about this: If you believe that something is
possible, even in your wildest dreams, it is a goal worth striving for.
The only qualification is that at some primary level you must believe
it is possible. You must be able to take it seriously even if you don't
imagine that anyone else can.

For example, if you're five feet four inches tall at the age of seventeen and in only average physical condition, it's probably self-
deluding to focus on becoming a star in the National Basketball
Association (NBA). That will not happen in this world or at least in
this lifetime. Even wanting it to happen is almost certainly a self-
serving fantasy of adulation that has nothing to do with really
improving your life. But while you may never score as many points
as Shaquille O'Neal, you *might* make as much money as Donald
Trump, provided that deep in your heart you really believe it's possible. You may not be ready to talk about that belief with anyone
else yet, but if it's there in your consciousness, it can be translated
into the real world. You just have to take the action that's required.

In this discussion we've touched on some of the possible challenges that you may be interposing between yourself and the true
purpose of your life. The items following define these challenges
more specifically. As you look them over, be aware that all of these
are internal issues. They don't refer to doing well in school or being
good looking or being popular. Every one of these problems is a self-
created mental, emotional, and spiritual obstacle. You brought them
into your life, and you can eliminate them. If these problems are
holding you back, you can change that right now.

"I don't believe—" When people don't believe they can get
what they really want, it's useful to ask what they do believe.

They believe their nightmares rather than their dreams. They
believe their doubts rather than their aspirations. But why? This
choice usually has less to do with objective realities than with
subjective doubts. Not believing really means believing too
much in the limited possibilities based on the present condition
of the ego. Whatever your ego tells you, you believe. Whatever
seems outside your ego cocoon, you choose not to believe in.
The solution? Put aside the whole concept of belief. Replace a
need to believe with a commitment to trust in the Light. Replace
the conditional power of belief with the unconditional power of
certainty.

"I'll have to work too hard—" This is another self-sabotaging
illusion. It's based on the idea that you have to endure pain to
deserve success. But happiness, like life itself and everything in
it, can never be deserved. These are God's gifts, not His com-
pensation to us for services rendered. Moreover, the concept of
deserving contains a hidden implication: if you can just suffer
enough to deserve something, then you're entitled to keep it.
When you realize that your true purpose is to be joyful, you
stop thinking about deserving.

"I'm not capable—" When you know that the sparks of God
are within you, you also know that your capabilities are unlimited, provided you reveal those sparks. The spiritual tools of
Kabbalah have been given to us to make that revelation possible. Every one of us has access to those tools. When we say, "I
can't do it," this doesn't express lack of trust in ourselves—it's
not trusting the great power that God has put within our grasp.
Whenever you feel that a task is too great for you, tell yourself:
"Yes, I'm not capable of meeting this challenge, but the Light
within me most definitely is capable of it." Then just go ahead.
Don't argue with yourself about the extent of your powers. The
power within you is unlimited.

"I'm afraid of being judged—" When you achieve your goals
(not if, but when), there will be people who respond negatively
to your joy. But there will be people who respond negatively no

matter what you do! Why do you let this negative energy influence your goals or any aspect of your life? Why do you think about someone else's negative energy when there are so many positive things that you can create? You'll be criticized in any case by people who appoint themselves to wear judicial robes. So what! You have more important things to think about!

CHAPTER FOUR

Netzach

From Victimhood to Victory

etzach is most often translated as victory. This means victory
over the negative forces within ourselves. It doesn't refer to
the triumph of an invading army, a natural disaster, or a physical handicap. Those things are significant only to the extent that
they affect our thoughts and emotions. Some people are affected
very deeply by external events, some much less so, and some not at
all. For everyone, however, these inner forces and nothing else prevent us from connecting directly with God.

The wisdom of God expresses itself in an infinite number of
ways: in the beauty of nature, in the love we feel for other living
things, and in the computers and cell phones that have brought
people so much closer together across the world. Though it's not
often easy, we should also realize how things that seem difficult and
even dangerous can also reveal wisdom, though at first it may be
beyond our understanding. This is not to say that when a problem—
or even a tragedy—arises in our lives, we need to convince ourselves
that it's somehow a good thing. It does mean, however, that God
always desires what's best for us. Part of our spiritual work is to be
aware of that truth, no matter what happens.

The Bible tells us that Moses spoke directly with God on Mount
Sinai. In Kabbalistic terms, this means that Moses had reached the
spiritual level of Netzach. He was capable of receiving divine

wisdom directly from its source, and he was also able to bring that wisdom to the people of Israel. Moses had become the supreme tzaddik, a person whose capacity to accept and to give wisdom was completely without boundaries.

While there may be no one equal to Moses on Earth today, certainly human beings can be found for whom ordinary limits don't seem to exist. There's so much we can learn from these people. There are children, for example, who can immediately play a musical instrument at an expert level, though they've never had a single lesson. Others can perform difficult mathematical calculations although they've been diagnosed with severe mental retardation. Science is unable to explain how this is possible—but it may be that musical, mathematical, or other talents represent the absence of inner blockages or inhibitions, rather than the presence of extraordinary gifts. Instead of wondering why some people are able to do amazing things, we should ask why all of us can't. Or maybe we can, once we get past the inner barriers that separate us from our truly unlimited potential.

—ᴄᴠ—

In order to win a war—remember, Netzach means victory—it's sometimes necessary to lose a battle or to pretend to lose one.

The Failing Student

Long ago, in what is now Russia, a young boy suddenly became very ill. He was a truly wonderful child, and his father was terribly upset. Not only was the boy a generous and truly good hearted person, but he was also a diligent student of the Bible and its mystical interpretations, which were known as Kabbalah. Sometimes, as tradition dictated, the boy and an elderly master of Kabbalah would meet at midnight to read the ancient teachings. In those days, Jewish parents valued learning and scholarship in their children above all else. The boy's father would stand watching, full of wonder and pride at his son's ability as a scholar.

But this boy also seemed special in many other ways. He was a kind and generous young man who went out of his way to help anyone who needed him. Yet now he was very sick. The doctors seemed helpless, and as much as his father resisted even thinking of such a thing, it seemed as if the boy was about to die.

In desperation, the father sought out his son's elderly teacher, who had been his son's guide. "I beseech you," said the father. "Come with me to my home to pray for my son. You know what a good person he is. He lives for others. He wants nothing for himself."

The sage listened closely and agreed to accompany the father to his home. There, as they stood beside the bedside of the dying boy, the father once again began to describe his son's virtues and to lament the great injustice of his imminent loss. Suddenly he looked sharply at the teacher standing beside him. "Aren't you going to pray for my son?" the father demanded. "You know him as well as I do. You know he's a wonderful young man who deserves to live!"

But the teacher only sighed. "It's true that I know your son very well," he said. "But I have to be honest. He's not as good a person as you think he is. He's actually a bit selfish. He doesn't really study the way he's supposed to. He doesn't pray that often either. Also, as a scholar of Kabbalah he leaves something to be desired. He often gets Noah mixed up with Moses, and he confuses the Golden Calf with the Red Heifer."

The sick boy's father could hardly believe what he was hearing. No one had ever said anything like this about his son. What's more, the criticism was coming from a man reputed to have great spiritual power. It was said that "the words of his mouth went straight to God's ear."

"You're condemning my son to death! Get out of my house!" the father shouted, and he slammed the door shut as the great teacher departed. But when he turned around, he saw that something very unexpected had happened. His son's eyes were open. His face looked alert. For the first time in days, it looked like recovery might be possible. Yet just a moment earlier, however, the slanderous words of the old teacher seemed to have sealed the boy's fate.

But when the father told his son what had happened, the boy immediately understood. "When you came to my teacher, you told him I was perfect, that I do everything right, down to the smallest detail. But if I'm perfect, why am I still in this world? What is there left for me to do? By all rights, God should take me. So my teacher said, 'No, he's not perfect. He has a lot of work left to do. He needs to stay in the world in order to accomplish the purpose for which he came.'" And the son recovered.

There are times when life can seem overwhelming. It may not really be a matter of life and death—but it definitely seems that way.

The Love Note

Jen shared a room with Katy, her older sister. Sometimes she really liked it. She was able to hear Katy talk on the phone, for one thing. But every year Katy seemed to have more freedom, and every year Jen still felt stuck in her role as "the younger one" who wasn't allowed to do anything. But that didn't stop her from trying.

One evening Jen was trying, sort of, to concentrate on writing a history report about the Boston Tea Party. Just then, a note from Steve (sigh!) fell out of her history book. Katy grabbed it.

"Hey, that's mine!" Jen said.

"Let me read it."

"No!"

"Why not?"

"Cause it's private, Katy."

"Jen, I tell you everything. And you get to hear even more. Do you want me to leave the room when I'm talking on the phone? Do you not want to know anything anymore about what I'm doing?"

Jen thought it over. "Okay. You can read it."

Katy opened the note.

Dear Jen:

Why did you shy away from me in the stairwell? That one time I got a few seconds alone with you was so special. You wouldn't kiss me, but a real girlfriend would have. I know you will soon and maybe more. I thought you wanted me. From the first time I met you, I knew you'd be mine. You are the girl of my dreams. You have everything— your looks, your personality. You will be popular real soon, especially if you are my girlfriend. But you are, aren't you? Don't you think of me at night? I think of you as mine and I expect a kiss next time I see you. Don't you think you owe me that to show me you like me? Don't you want to? How do I even know if you really like me? You haven't given me any proof. If you won't, I won't bother you anymore. I'll ignore you in the hallway when I see you in school. Please be mine—and—if you want to be mine— prove it. I'll be dreaming of you and the last time we were alone together.

Steve

Katy looked up from the letter. "Whoa," she said, then looked at Jen concerned. "You really like him a lot, don't you?"

"Uh-huh."

"Jen, I know what he's doing. It's so easy for me to see it."

"To see what? Why can't I have a boyfriend? I didn't even do any-thing with him!"

"No, but you're thinking about it, and he's pressuring you. It's so obvious to me, but you don't see it. He's trying to make you do more and to give him more than you want to give. The next time you see him, you'll give in to him, cater to him. You'll want to prove you're his girlfriend. This is pressure he's putting on you, and I don't like it and neither should you!"

"But what do I do? I do like him."

"Write him a note back. Set him straight."

"But, Jen, I don't want to lose him."

"You won't lose him if you're smart—unless he's a total jerk. Be wary, be noncommittal, and most of all, don't show your weakness. Show your strength. Balance the two. It's up to you, Jen. Show him your limits without showing him exactly how you feel."

Jen thought about it. Her sister seemed right. But she was not about to lose this guy. He was the love of her life! So the next day she wrote a reply.

Dear Steve:

I think you're going too fast. We just met and we're not even in the 11th grade. What do you think I can "give" you? Yes, I think of you and sometimes I think of us as boyfriend and girlfriend in the future. Steve, I think of me also and of what I can do and cannot do. You want me to prove I'm your girlfriend, well, you've never said that but in a note. We've never even dated. As much as I don't want to lose you, I don't think you've given me enough cause to stay around and "prove" to you, as you roughly put it, that I'm not your girlfriend. If you want to respect me and date me, why the pressure? If I've the personality and looks you want, why don't you wait for me? Is there someone on the sidelines who you absolutely need to be with? Then why try so hard for me. Steve, it's not like we've been dating for six months. This is new. I think I'm worth waiting for. Don't you? At this point, why do I have to prove I'm your girlfriend? Also, I have limitations, and I have expectations also, Steve. Don't underestimate me.

Jen

Jen rewrote the note several times, keeping it carefully hidden from Katy. But really, she wanted to show her sister what she'd written. In fact, someday she would probably have to show her, so she decided to do it now. Katy could be a pain, but she was also very smart. Or maybe she was just older. Whatever. Jen showed her the note.

Katy read it, then looked up and smiled. "Wow, Jen, there are some good lines here. But you sound so innocent, so—*naïve*. Let's redo this. Let's, uh, reel him in!"

So Katy revised the note:

Steve,

You are going way too fast. We just met and we're not even in the 11th grade and now I'm supposed to be your girlfriend already. I will "give" you what a girlfriend gives you when I'm ready and not before. Yes, I think of you at night. A lot. And sometimes I think of us as boyfriend and girlfriend in the future. Steve, I think of me also and of what I can do and cannot do. You want me to prove I'm your girlfriend, well, you've never said that but in a note. We've never even dated. If I'm going to be popular, I will. When I am, no one will put this much pressure on me. I will rule! Ha ha! As much as I don't want to lose you, I don't think you've given me enough cause to stay around and "prove" to you, as you roughly put it, that I'm your girlfriend. If you want to respect me and date me, why the pressure? If I've the personality and looks you want, why don't you wait for me? It's not like we're out of time. I'm sure there is no bet going on with your friends as to how soon it would be before I "caved" to your wishes and you won the bet. Yep, I'm sure there is no bet. So, is there someone on the sidelines who you absolutely need to be with? Then why try so hard for me. Steve, it's not like we've been dating for six months. This is new. I think I'm worth waiting for. Don't you? At this point, why do I have

to prove I'm your girlfriend? Why don't you prove you
want me to be just that? I have limitations, and also I have
expectations, Steve. What about what I need from you? No
pressure. Stop pushing me forward. If it's meant to be and
I want you, wait for me to come to you, and most of all,
don't underestimate me.

Jen

As Jen read the note, everything that had taken place in the last
week flashed before her eyes. She had met Steve Nevins, in the hallway. Well, he met her. He was at Jen's locker. He put his arm above
her and her open locker, so she couldn't get away. Jen knew she was
blushing, but tried to be really cool, like this was no big deal.

"Hi there," he said.

"Hi."

"My name's Steve."

"Yeah. I've heard about you."

"Really? Good things, I hope."

"I'll never tell."

He put his arm down. "Well, I gotta go."

"Okay. Bye."

"Bye."

That was it. But then Steve kept flirting with Jen over the next
few days. Finally he tried to kiss her in the back stairwell of the
school, which was where such things often went on. But Jen got out
of there fast. Then she told her friend about it. She told Pam that it
had kind of freaked her out.

"Well," Pam asked, "what were you doing in the stairwell in the
first place?"

Jen didn't really have an answer.

Now, after reading her sister's rewrite of her note, Jen folded it
and put it into her history book. Should she put it in Steve's locker?
Or should she talk to Steve directly? Maybe she should just forget

about the note. In fact, maybe she should just forget about Steve. Maybe she should ask her parents if she could move into another room. Maybe she should also ask if she could transfer to another school. Maybe they weren't even her real parents. She might have been adopted, and they had never told her. Everything suddenly seemed so complicated. Nothing seemed certain anymore. Absolutely nothing.

—∾—

Netzach Summary

It's hard to appreciate the good qualities of people who are closest to us. It's much easier to admire people who live in some faraway country or who lived in the past or whom we see in a movie about some planet in a distant galaxy. But if you do a bit of research, you'll find that even the most admirable individuals were not considered admirable in their own time. In fact, it was usually just the opposite, and this is certainly true of the heroes and heroines of Kabbalistic teachings.

The people of Israel, for example, wanted to kill Moses. This may seem strange, since he was the person who led them out of slavery in Egypt—but that's the reason they wanted to kill him! He had taken the people from the bondage in which they were miserable to the freedom in which they felt frightened and uncertain. Although the people now had the potential to find fulfillment in their lives, they had moments when they preferred the prisoners' life, in which they did not have to take any responsibility for their own well-being. If something went wrong, they could blame it on the Egyptians—and they could feel sorry for themselves too!

The great teachers of Kabbalah were also subjected to anger and persecution. Rabbi Shimon bar Yochai lived in the second century A.D., when the Romans governed what is now the nation of Israel.

According to the teachings of Kabbalah, Moses himself gave Rabbi Shimon the text of the Zohar, the great book of Kabbalistic wisdom.

Rabbi Shimon had a school for the study of the Bible and its commentaries, but the Romans had outlawed Bible study. As a result, Rabbi Shimon hid for thirteen years in the mountains. It was there that Moses appeared to him.

There's no question that Rabbi Shimon was persecuted. It's important to realize, however, that being a target of persecution is not the same as being a victim of it. Kabbalah teaches that the role of victim is always a choice. It can never be imposed from the outside.

Sometimes, when people learn that rejecting the victim mentality is such an important precept of Kabbalah, they begin to take offense. Does this mean, for example, that it's your fault whenever something bad happens? Does it mean that you've somehow chosen to have a serious illness in your own life or in your family? Does it mean that homeless people are somehow at fault for what their lives are like? Does it mean that people who perished in Nazi concentration camps were somehow responsible for their own murder?

Actually, none of these things are true. When something painful or dangerous comes into your life, it's not because you've chosen for that to happen. But once it does happen, the choice is always yours as to how you'll respond. It was not Moses' "fault" that people turned against him, nor was it because of something Rabbi Shimon had done that he had to hide in the cave. These things were not punishments. Instead, they were challenges, and they were even opportunities. They were times in which people with great souls could really show what they were made of. Moses led his people out of the desert.

So when the world seems to be against you, the teachings of Kabbalah are very clear: first, refuse to see yourself as a victim; second, recognize that adversity can be a chance to demonstrate and develop strength; and finally, take action to show your understanding of these two principles.

None of this is easy, and it even gets a bit harder. Kabbalah teaches that it's not enough to act positively when things go wrong. Your *motivation* for positive action is just as important as the action itself. When people don't seem to notice you, for example, you may find yourself doing things just to gain their appreciation. From a Kabbalistic perspective, this short-circuits the positive energy of the action. The tzaddikim—the great souls of the Bible and of Kabbalistic legends—never wanted or expected anything in return. They knew that if they directed their energy toward getting something from the people around them—even if it was the love and admiration that they completely deserved—they'd sacrifice their connection to God.

In order to understand this, we must remember how the Kabbalists have defined the ultimate purpose. That purpose is not to get rich or famous or popular. It is simply to develop the full and unlimited potential of our souls so that we can receive the happiness that is intended for us. It is to get outside of our comfort zone into new territory that provides room in which we can grow. Usually there is some difficulty associated with that experience, and often there is even some pain.

In the stories you've just read, this difficulty appears in two very different ways. In the first story, a father is faced with the imminent death of his son. In the second, a girl tries to deal with her attraction for a boy in her high school. These are two very different situations, in two very different periods of history. At a glance, the father's problem might seem much more serious than the girl's, yet both people feel overwhelmed by what life has brought to them. The truth is, however, that the pain they feel isn't dependent on the external situation. It's dependent on their responses to the situation. What's more, our responses are always within our control, if we're just willing to accept that responsibility to reject the role of victim once and for all. As we've said earlier, this is not easy, and you may not see "results" right away.

There is a Hebrew phrase that describes the best way to look at our own positive actions. Literally translated, the phrase means "You won't see the reward in this lifetime." In one sense, this refers to reincarnation, which definitely is a basic Kabbalistic concept. But it has another meaning as well: that we won't gain the benefits of the right action until we transform ourselves at the most basic level—until we begin living "another lifetime" even while we still inhabit the same body. We will not gain the benefits of living according to Kabbalistic teachings until we change ourselves into a vessel that is fully able to receive those gifts.

CHAPTER FIVE

Gevurah

The Power of Judgment

In Kabbalisitc teachings, the concept of judgment isn't connected with blame or guilt. Instead, it's closer to a principle of science: for every action, there's a reaction. This is as true in human life as it is in physics.

Kabbalah teaches that God's only desire is to bestow his love on us. But what does this really mean? There is no simple answer. Even when parents love their children, there are still moments in which the children need to be corrected or re-directed. This is not the same thing as "punishment." It is really a matter of returning the child to the correct path. To the child, this may initially be perceived as difficult or even painful. But if even greater difficulty and pain are to be avoided in the future, sometimes they have to be confronted in the present.

To understand the energy of judgment, you must remember that Kabbalah generally avoids words such as "good" or "bad." Instead, thoughts, feelings, and actions can be positive in one setting and negative in another, or negative to the recipient and positive to the giver. Sometimes, for example, it may be very positive for a grandparent to give candy to a child—positive for both the giver and the receiver. But sometimes it may be positive for only one of them or, perhaps, for even neither of them. It is all a matter of the intention and the purpose that underlie the physical action.

There may be days, for example, when you really don't feel like studying for school. There may also be times when you feel like eating nothing but junk food or watching television all day long. What is the best response to these feelings? Should you *always* let yourself do what you want in the moment that you want it? Should you *never* let yourself do what you want? How can you balance the conflicts that sometimes come up between what you desire right now and what you want for yourself tomorrow or next year or even over the course of your life?

If you think about it for a moment, you will see that the positive or negative of doing anything can vary according to the goals of the person who performs the action. A kidnapper may use a candy bar to lure a child into a car. A doctor may also try to cheer up a young patient by offering her a candy bar. So can we conclude that giving candy to a child is bad—or is it good?

There is no right answer, because the intentions and the situation are never exactly alike. At least, they are never alike for human beings, but God's circumstances never change, nor do his intentions. No matter what God brings into our lives, his intention is to draw us closer to him. This does not mean closer in a physical sense because God is everywhere, but closer to his essential nature, which is to have no needs of his own and to give and to share of himself.

In considering this, you might have the impression that Kabbalah is about becoming a saintly person—that it focuses on the need to give up your own desires in order to benefit others. In a sense, that's correct, but our own self-interest is really the foundation of all Kabbalistic teaching. In today's world, we're taught that fulfillment comes with material success. The more money we make, the more possessions we accumulate, the happier we'll be. Kabbalah doesn't say that we shouldn't be interested in material success. It does say, however, that material success is not, and can never be, the source of real joy in life. Strange as it may seem, the only way we can really get what we want and need is by giving to others. Getting is fine, but getting in order to give takes us beyond the limits of material existence and brings us closer to the ultimate freedom of God.

Let us try to sum this up. Two equal and opposite forms of energy are present throughout the universe. One is the power of kindness and mercy. The other is the power of justice—of action and reaction. To be a complete human being, both these energies must be available to our consciousness and active in our daily lives. We must recognize the need for both gentleness and firmness. We must be able to use both of them in our dealings with other people, and we must accept the fact that they will be applied to us as well.

For most people, it is easier to judge than to be judged. While it may be painful to recognize the shortcomings of those we love and care about, it's even more painful to see where we ourselves have been less than perfect—sometimes far less. But we cannot be complete human beings until we acknowledge the need for judgment. We cannot fulfill our mission of developing ourselves to the fullest unless we are able to judge others fairly and are equally able to accept fair judgment of ourselves.

This is the true meaning of the story of Abraham and Isaac presented here. It's one of the most controversial and misunderstood of all the biblical tales. For centuries, critics of traditional religion have referred to this story as an example of God's essential cruelty and selfishness. "If God is supposed to be a father," they have asked, "what kind of father would order another father to sacrifice his child? How can anyone worship such a mean-spirited, bloodthirsty God?"

If we limit ourselves to the words of the story itself, it does indeed seem as if God has crossed over into genuinely cruel behavior. First, he made Abraham and Sarah wait many years for the birth of their child, and then he ordered the murder of that very child. And the fact that God relented at the last moment changes nothing. If someone holds a gun to another person's head and then pulls the trigger, this is still criminal behavior even if it turns out that the gun isn't loaded. To say, "Just kidding!" is not a good excuse.

But Kabbalah's interpretation of the story involves more than what's on the page. The entire Bible, according to Kabbalistic teaching, is really a coded document that must be understood in symbolic terms. A literal reading of the Bible—the kind of reading that depicts God as a cruel manipulator—can only lead us to the opposite of the truth. In fact, the Talmud and the Zohar explicitly state that trying to understand the Bible in literal terms is not just a mistake, but a major sin.

So how should we understand the story of Isaac's near sacrifice? There are three important points to be made. First, we must understand Abraham's special relationship with God: they go way back! From the day that He first told Abraham that he would be the founder of a great nation, God tested him again and again. Some of these tests are described in the Bible itself—as when Abraham was called on to offer Isaac as a sacrifice—and there are many more stories of this kind in the biblical commentaries. To prepare Abraham to be the patriarch, or father, of the Jewish people, he was put in situations that would have broken the faith of anyone except a most devoted servant of the Lord. But God not only put Abraham *in* these situations, however, but he also got Abraham *out* of them. Or rather, Abraham got himself out of them based on his unwavering belief in the love and goodness of the Lord.

With these events in the background, we can ask ourselves what might have been going through Abraham's mind when God told him to take his son to Mount Moriah. On the one hand, Abraham must have been startled and frightened by this command. He must have asked himself the same question that scholars have asked through the centuries. How could God do such a thing? In fact, a strong argument could be made that, from Abraham's point of view, the question contained its own answer. God couldn't do such a thing. There must be something else going on here. There must be some hidden reason for God to command this terrible deed—a reason, perhaps, that no human being is worthy to know, but a reason that would certainly become clear at the proper time and place.

On a less philosophical level, there are other hints that God's order was less straightforward than it might seem. By this time in his life, Abraham had certainly learned to listen closely to whatever God said. He would probably have noticed, therefore, that God didn't just say, "Sacrifice your son to me." Instead, he said, "Offer your son as a sacrifice," which is something very different. Just because we're told to make the offering of a sacrifice, that doesn't necessarily mean we'll have to make the sacrifice itself. Perhaps Abraham was aware of this distinction as he heard God's command. Perhaps Abraham knew that this was yet another test, like the patience he had been called on to show in the many years when he and his wife had not been able to have a child. This was a harder test, a test that was more difficult to understand, but a test that he could pass in the same way that he'd passed all the others, by keeping his faith in God.

So perhaps Abraham secretly knew that God would never "go through with it," or perhaps he thought that, for whatever unknowable reason, God really would call on him to sacrifice his child. In any case, Abraham proceeded to do as he was told. It couldn't have been easy, because as the story makes clear, Abraham was a thoroughly gentle, kind, and merciful human being. It was completely unlike him to do violence or bring harm on anybody, especially his own son. But he was prepared to do it if need be, even though it was completely against his nature.

Actually, the fact that it was against Abraham's nature is the key to the whole story from a Kabbalistic point of view. To understand this, we must remember the fundamental reason we are in the world. It isn't to become rich or powerful. It isn't even to become wise. It isn't even to become good. Instead, we're here to expand our souls to their full potential because in doing so we can become like God. In fact, the ancient Kabbalists teach that we'll literally become God—a being who *lacks nothing*—when we've brought our souls through all ten levels of energy that are described in this book.

There is no doubt that Abraham was a good person. In fact, he was a "perfect" human being in terms of the goodness and kindness that shone through his every gesture. But he was not a complete human being in the Kabbalistic sense. Precisely because of his gentle and loving nature, he lacked the energy of judgment and force that is also an aspect of God. When the Lord called on Abraham to offer Isaac as a sacrifice, he challenged Abraham to go beyond what he was, and even beyond what he wanted to be. He forced Abraham to go beyond his limits in order to bring another form of divine power into Abraham's soul—that is, the power of judgment as we have described it.

This teaching has some very practical applications for how we live our lives. Repeatedly in the Bible and in other tales of Kabbalah, we meet people who are incomplete in one way or another, and this incompleteness is a much more fundamental characteristic than whether they are good or bad. The task of these people (and our task too) is not really to become better, but to become more *ourselves*, more of whom we really are as unique human beings. In this way we can become one with God, which is the ultimate objective of every soul.

As you read the second story in this section, think about the girl who steals the watch. Suppose her father had been a thoroughly kind and gentle person—someone like Abraham had been, someone who "wouldn't hurt a fly." In that case, even when his daughter stole the watch, he might have found it impossible to cause her any pain. Even if it were for her own good, the energy of judgment would simply not be available to him. If that were the case, he would never have made her wear the watch for a year as a reminder of what she had done, even if it would have prevented her from making the same mistake in the future. Instead, he would have forgiven her at the outset. This would have saved the father from feeling any pain. This would have allowed him to stay within his "comfort zone." But it would not have been what was best for his daughter. It would have been an expression of his soul's own limits, and it would have passed those limits on to her.

Sometimes we must do things that cause discomfort to others, but Kabbalah teaches that this is justified as long as our ultimate intentions are correct. This is the real meaning of judgment. On the other hand, failure to render judgment in order to keep feeling good about ourselves is nothing but a subtle form of selfishness.

In the story of Abraham and his son, Isaac certainly seems to understand this. He knows that "something is up," and he seems to know that it might be something unpleasant. In fact, in other versions of the story, Abraham explicitly tells Isaac that God has commanded his sacrifice, and Isaac accepts the command just as his father had. In fact, Isaac actually helps to prepare the sacrificial fire.

Needless to say, it isn't always easy to be this agreeable when a parent seems to be doing something that makes no sense or that even causes us some pain. In today's world, in fact, there are times when you definitely should resist parental actions that are obviously dangerous or hurtful. But it's usually clear that parents have our best interests at heart, even if this causes some short-term discomfort.

So connecting with the energy of judgment is a very important task. In various ways, first as sons or daughters and later as parents, it's a job that continues throughout our lives. Judgment, however, is an especially difficult energy to control. When you feel inclined to deal firmly or even severely with another person, always look carefully at what you're about to do and why you want to do it. If it's for your own self-interest or self-satisfaction, resist this temptation. Are you taking action because it will make you feel better or because you truly believe it's best for everyone involved. If you sincerely believe that your action will be beneficial in the long run—for other people as well as yourself—then go ahead. But remember: There will be occasions when *you* will be the object of someone's judgment. Accept those occasions with the same positive intentions that you judge others.

—ɯ—

This following story is one of the best-known tales in the Bible. It's also one of the most controversial—and misunderstood.

The Binding of Isaac

The Bible tells us that Abraham was a thoroughly kind and loving person. His whole life was dedicated, first, to doing God's will, and second, to helping people. He never hesitated to put the needs of others above his own desires.

When Abraham was ninety-seven years old, God spoke to him and told him that he would be the father of a great nation. This may have seemed a bit hard to believe, since Abraham and Sarah, his wife, had not even had one child. But Abraham trusted in God. If God said that his descendants would be as plentiful as the stars in the sky, Abraham was sure that this destiny would be fulfilled. Still, many years passed and Abraham and Sarah had no children.

Finally, when both Abraham and Sarah had reached the age of almost one hundred years, God told them that a miracle was about to happen: they would have a son. Sarah doubted this could be possible. In fact, she laughed when God made the announcement. Abraham's faith never wavered, however, and it happened. Sarah gave birth to a boy. They named him *Isaac*, which is derived from the Hebrew word for "laughter," because Sarah had laughed when God told her she would finally become a parent.

Now that he had a son, perhaps God's prophecy would finally come true. Perhaps Abraham's descendants really would become a great nation. But then, when Isaac had grown into a young man, something truly astounding happened.

God spoke to Abraham again. He said, "Take your son and offer him to me as a burnt sacrifice."

How could this be possible? First God had told Abraham that he and his wife would have many thousands of descendants. Then they were not granted even one child until they were deep into old age. And now, after all they'd been through, God told Abraham to offer Isaac as a sacrifice. Could there possibly be any explanation for this? God offered none.

It would have been a terribly cruel blow to anyone, but this command was especially difficult for Abraham. It was not in his nature to bring harm to anyone and, certainly, not to his only son. God was telling Abraham to do something that was completely contrary to the kind of person he had always tried to be. What could Abraham have thought about this? He had always trusted God in the past, but this was the most difficult test of his faith. It seemed to turn everything else God had said into a cruel joke.

Still, Abraham prepared to do as God had ordered him. In those days it was the custom of many religions to sacrifice sheep or birds. Usually the animal would be quickly killed with a sharp knife, and then its body would be burned on a pyre of twigs and branches. Abraham spoke to Isaac and said that they would be going into the desert to make such a sacrifice. He even asked Isaac to help him collect wood for the sacrificial fire. Isaac helped his father load some wood onto the back of a donkey. Then, together with a servant, they set out for the mountain called Moriah, where sacrifices were traditionally carried out.

As they approached the mountain, it occurred to Isaac that something might be wrong. "Father," he said to Abraham, "where is the animal that we will sacrifice to God?"

"God will provide the animal," Abraham answered simply. By now the mountain was clearly in view. "Isaac, look there, up to the top of the mountain," Abraham said. "Tell me what you see."

Isaac did as Abraham asked, and a look of amazement came over his face. "I see a huge pillar of fire!" he said. "Surely some sort of great miracle is going to happen up there."

Abraham nodded. "Yes, I also see the pillar of fire," he told Isaac. "So you and I will go up to the top of the mountain together."

A short distance away, the servant was standing with the donkey. Now Abraham approached the servant and spoke to him just as he had spoken to Isaac. "Look there, up to the top of the mountain," he said. "Tell me what you see."

The servant looked, and the expression on his face remained unchanged. "I don't see anything unusual," he said. "Just the top of the mountain."

Once again, Abraham nodded. "Yes, and the donkey doesn't see anything unusual either. So you should stay here with the donkey."

Then, carrying wood for the sacrificial fire, Abraham and Isaac began their climb up the mountain. There are several versions of what happened when they got to the top.

According to some accounts, as Abraham began to make a pile the wood, Isaac said, "Father, we have wood for the fire, but where is the animal that will be the sacrifice?" And Abraham replied, "God will provide it." Clearly, in this rendition of the story, Isaac does not realize that he himself will be offered to God. In other versions, Isaac not only knew what was about to happen, but he took part voluntarily in preparing the wood and unhesitatingly had lain down on top of it. Here Isaac is presented not as a naïve victim, but as a spiritually developed human being whose faith in God is equal to that of his father.

After the wood was in order in the form of a sacrificial altar, Abraham bound Isaac and drew a knife. What was going through his mind at this moment? Did he suspect that God would actually allow him to go through with the ritual murder of his only son? Or did he still believe that, for reasons that were unclear, God was testing him, seeing how far he could go, until the very last moment. What could Isaac have been thinking? Was he completely passive, mystified by what was being done to him? Or was he, like his father, actively prepared to do whatever was required to show his faith in God's judgment.

One thing is certain in all versions of the story: Isaac survived, although just barely. At the very last instant, an angel appeared and turned the knife away as Abraham was about to plunge it into Isaac's throat. Then the angel revealed a ram whose horns had become entangled in a nearby bush. Rather than sacrificing Isaac, Abraham could offer the ram.

As you might expect, this was not an entirely satisfactory ending from Abraham's point of view. In fact, we are told that he directly confronted God and demanded an explanation.

"When one person tempts or tests another person," Abraham said, "it's to find out what is in his heart. But surely you already knew what was in my heart. You knew that I was even ready to sacrifice my son!"

God had to agree. "Yes, it was known to me."

"Then why did you do this to me?" Abraham demanded.

"I did it for two reasons," God said. "First, because I wanted you to reveal an aspect of your devotion that has never been revealed before—your power to do even things that are against your nature if I demand it of you. Second, I wanted others to see this. I wanted the world to see the kind of person I chose to be the father of the nation of Israel."

Hearing this, Abraham almost laughed out loud. "Did you not promise me that my descendants would be as numberless as the stars in the sky?"

"Yes, I did."

"And is not Isaac the first of those descendants?"

"Yes."

"Yet you directed me to offer him as a sacrifice! And when you did so, I could have refused. I could have declared that you were breaking your promise to me made so many years ago, for which I waited so patiently for you to fulfill—the promise that I would be the founder of a great nation. But I did as you asked. Therefore I now have something to ask of you. When my descendants commit any sin against you, remember what I was prepared to do on your behalf, and forgive them."

God listened and then replied, "I will forgive them when mercy and kindness are just, but I cannot forgive them when justice and judgment are needed. Only on New Year's day will I forgive all transgressions, no matter how grave. I demand only that the ram's horn be sounded, to commemorate the ram that I sent in place of Isaac's sacrifice."

To this day, when a ram's horn is sounded in the synagogue during the New Year's celebration, all sins are forgiven.

—⟋⟍—

The energy of judgment is most powerful when it originates within yourself. That's the theme of the story that follows.

The Thief

Whenever I went out with my friends, one of them always had something new to show off. Once, Sandy had a dark brown leather and suede purse—a designer original no less. Another time, Dorie's nails were done extra long. Her parents let her. (Dorie has cool parents.) And then Jill had her hair streaked red and blonde. Whatever. They always had something to talk about.

Sometimes I wondered if my family was really poor. It didn't seem like we had as much money as other people. Whenever we went shopping, which wasn't that often, I always got what I needed, but not much more. I hardly ever got anything to show off. And when I did a few times, Sandy or Dorie or Jill would "top" me with the latest purchases that their parents let them get. It was tough to compete, so mostly I kept quiet.

One day my mom took me shopping at Costco. I wanted to go to the mall where they have better stuff, but she said we needed to save money. "Costco has what you need," she told me. (Yeah, and how about what I want?)

Well, she bought me some socks and a pair of shoes and some towels and about a month's worth of frozen meat. Then, amazingly, she stopped as we were passing the jewelry department. "I need to get a pair of earrings," she said. And guess what? That meant she'd buy me a pair too.

Over the next half hour the sales guy brought out almost every earring tree and every velvet box of post earrings in the whole store. We tried on lots of them. Then for some reason he started showing us some brightly colored Swatch watches to match the earrings. One watch was really cool, with an ice-blue face. Others had reproductions of famous paintings, like the Mona Lisa. Very cool. Very sophisticated. Lots of kids walk around with dumb stuff from movies and music videos—but a watch with a famous painting was really something different.

The sad part was, I knew she'd never get it for me. Even if I said I didn't want any earrings and wanted the watch instead, she would never go for it. That's just the way she was. We came in there to buy earrings—which was pretty amazing in itself—so we couldn't buy watches.

But I really wanted that watch! "Should I make a scene?" I thought to myself. "Should I scream, plead, and cry?" I considered it. But, really, it wouldn't have done any good. So I didn't say anything at all. But I couldn't stop looking at that Mona Lisa watch. Totally cool.

Well, at least I got some earrings. Back home I put them in my jewelry box, but it was almost hard to look at them because they would have gone so well with that artsy watch. I even got an art book down from the bookshelf to look at the Mona Lisa again. What a great idea to put that on a watch! She looks so mysterious, which is kind of like how I like to look. Plus, it was bound to be a collector's item and become really valuable. Pretty soon you'd never be able to buy one. But would mom understand that? Would I be able to explain that to her? Would she even believe me? No way.

I made a decision. The next day I went back to Costco. Incredibly enough, just as I was about to leave my mom said, "Tracey, don't you like your new earrings?"

"Sure I like them!"

"Well, you're not wearing them."

"Oh, I just forgot." So I went back and put the earrings on, and then I left.

First I just walked around the store for a while. I was a little hesitant about going back to the jewelry counter, but finally I did. The same sales guy was there.

I said, "Hi. Remember yesterday when I was in here with my mom and we got these earrings? You were showing us some Swatch watches. Could I see those again?"

He was real friendly. "Sure. Which ones would you like to see?"

"Oh, I'd like to see a lot of them. Maybe even all of them. I'd like to see some more earrings too."

So he brought out a tray of earrings and some watches. I looked at them and then asked to see some more. He kept bringing stuff. Of course, he brought the Mona Lisa watch, too, but I pretended even not to notice it. I just picked out a cheap pair of earrings and paid for them.

Then, while he was ringing them up, I put the Swatch watch of my dreams into my purse. There was so much stuff on the counter that there was no way he could notice. Plus, when he came back with the earrings, I chatted with him for a while so that it wouldn't look like I was trying to hurry out of there. Finally I left.

Out in the parking lot, I thought, "What if someone saw me? What if I'm being followed out here?" I walked fast. No! Slow down. If you run, they'll know you're guilty. Finally, I made it to my car and quickly drove out of there.

"Honk!"

I slammed on the brakes. I had almost backed into a fat SUV. I'd better watch out! Why did I take that watch? What was I thinking? Now I would have to hide it from mom and dad. But for how long? Could I ever let them see it? Wait! I could say I bought it somewhere else. Somewhere cheap, a pawn shop maybe.

I pulled out of the parking lot. Then as I drove along, I noticed a bee on the windshield—actually, it was inside the windshield. I lowered the car windows. But the bee just flew around, finally landing on the steering wheel right next to my hands! I was scared stiff. If it stung me, I might get into an accident. But if I pulled over and tried to chase it out of the car, a cop might stop to see what's wrong and discover my stolen watch. Well, there was nothing to do but try to think good thoughts. The bee wouldn't sting a good person. But was I still a good person? I wondered. Maybe so. At least the bee flew out. Suddenly I noticed how the watch glowed when the sun hit it a certain way. It looked great on my wrist. My friends would be so envious!

I imagined it going like this: I'd let them do their "show and tell" thing with whatever stuff they'd bought. Then I'd casually let them notice the Swatch with the Mona Lisa image—a watch like none of them had even seen!

"Tracey, what's this?" Jill would say.

"Oh, just my new watch," I said.

"It's a Swatch!" Dorie would say. "I have several of them but I don't have that one!" Sandy wouldn't say anything. But maybe later she would offer to buy it from me.

By the time I got home I was on cloud nine again. I knew everything would be fine. I considered taking the watch off, but I couldn't bear to do it. So I kept it on right through dinner. No problems! In fact, I was a little disappointed that neither mom nor dad even seemed to notice anything different. But later dad walked into my room. I was at my desk doing some homework, and he took me completely by surprise.

"Nice watch," he said.

"Oh, thanks!"

"Where'd you get it?"

"A pawn shop."

"The sales guy from Costco called."

My heart skipped a beat. "Really? What did he say?"

"He said he saw you yesterday with Mom and you bought earrings. Then you came by today and a Swatch watch was gone after you left. He had mom's credit card receipt, so he got our phone number."

He gave me a look that said, "I know you took it, so don't even think about lying to me."

My eyes filled with tears. "Dad, I'll give it back! I don't even want it! I mean, I was planning to pay for it later when I had enough money." I was blabbing on and on. "I'll return it tomorrow!"

"No. I want you to keep it," he said. "I've taken care of the bill."

"But I don't want it!"

"That's why I want you to keep it!" he said sharply.

Now I was totally confused. He sat down on the bed. "I want you to wear that watch every day for one full year."

I didn't know what to say. I just sat there. All of a sudden the watch felt like it was made out of red-hot iron. I was actually frightened to look at it, just like I'd been frightened of the bee in the car that afternoon.

"Every time you look at it, you'll remember how you got it," he said. "I'll remember too. And so will your mother."

"She knows?"

"What do you think?" I didn't think anything. I just wanted to die.

After the year was over, I took the watch off and I never wore it again. There had been many times during the year when I'd wanted so badly to throw it away, but in the end I decided to keep it. It's in my jewelry box and I see it all the time. Sometimes I even pick it up and look at it for a while when I'm getting ready to go out with my friends.

—ɯ—

Gevurah Summary

Over the centuries, Kabbalah has come to be identified with the Jewish religion. There are certainly some good reasons for this. Only the Jewish people have explicitly made the word "Kabbalah" part of their observances and traditions. This is rather ironic, because the Kabbalists themselves have taught that Kabbalah transcends the limits of any religion and even the idea of religion itself. The teachings of Kabbalah, therefore, cannot be identified with Judaism or any other organized form of spiritual practice. Instead, Kabbalah should be seen as the basis of every form of spirituality. The great truths of Kabbalah can be found in any authentic religion.

To see what this means, consider the many almost identical stories and teachings that appear in various spiritual traditions. Some of these are very well known; the legend of a great flood, for instance, is found in many cultures. Another somewhat lesser known story is also told throughout the world, and it perfectly expresses the meaning of judgment—what it is and what it isn't. It's one of the many fables in which a spiritual traveler is given permission to visit the next world and then return to the realm of the living.

In this fable, an angel offers to show the traveler both heaven and hell. Together they walk through a doorway into a huge banquet hall in which people are seated around a table laden with every kind of food and drink. Many people are seated around the table, but despite the presence of so much food, they all seem close to starvation. The reason for this soon becomes clear. Every one of the people at the table has a long spoon attached to each of their wrists, but the shafts of the spoons are so long that the famished diners are unable to put anything into their mouths. Wonderful things to eat surround them, but it always remains out of their reach.

When the traveler has seen enough of this dismal spectacle, the angel offers to show him what heaven looks like. Once again they enter a banquet hall where the table is piled high with food. Once again people around the table have long-shafted spoons attached to their wrists. But unlike the individuals in the first room, these people are extremely happy and well fed.

The reason is very simple: although the spoons make it impossible for them to feed themselves, they are just right for bringing food to the adjacent diners. By sharing with others instead of trying to provide only for themselves, the people in the second room have transformed their physical setting so that it has an entirely different effect.

And they've done this by themselves. The judgment of whether they'll be in heaven or in hell hasn't come from somewhere on high. It's entirely a function of their own consciousness. This is very important because the very idea of judgment seems to imply an external authority. But the idea of an external authority imposing a judgment on us is fundamentally contrary to Kabbalistic teaching. We bring energies of all kinds into our lives in the same way that radios or television sets attract different stations or frequencies. We're the ones who set the dial, and we can change that setting whenever we want. So as we make a change, the program that we attract is immediately altered.

If you feel you've been tried, convicted, and punished by "the universe," ask yourself whether it's easier to see yourself in that victim role than to take responsibility for what's happening in your life. Once you do this, you may realize that there's indeed something you deserve to be judged for, and you can then work through that process on your own. Or you may see that, for whatever reason, you're motivated to "beat yourself up." If that's the case, you can instantly give yourself a reprieve by connecting to the next of the Kabbalistic Sefirot.

CHAPTER SIX

Chesed

Strength Through Kindness

hesed can be translated as mercy, kindness, or benevolence. Ultimately, however, it's the energy of love that wants only to give of itself and that asks nothing in return. According to Kabbalistic teaching, this is literally the energy that created the world. But for the same reason it's not all that's required for the world to receive everything that the Creator has to give.

Why are we here? Is the existence of the universe simply the result of some cosmic accident and huge statistical improbability? Or has it come about through the intentional design of a supernatural being? If you choose to believe the first explanation, you have plenty of impressive company. This, after all, represents the current thinking of mainstream science and cosmology. But let's suppose you're interested at least in exploring the second perspective; that is, the existence of a God whose energy and intelligence underlie all material reality.

As a first step in this exploration, you might ask why God went to all the trouble. If God is truly a supreme being, he can presumably "do whatever he wants." So why did he want to create the world? What was in it for him? To answer this, we have to understand the difference between God's desires and our own wants and needs. What, after all, can God really want? A new car? A better job? Admission to an elite college? The very idea of God having ordinary human desires is nothing less than comical. On the other hand, if God has no desires at all, then nothing at all will happen because God by definition is the basis for all reality.

If we think about it logically, we will realize that there's only one desire—or perhaps even a need—that God can have. Since he can't lack anything, he can't really want to get anything. But since he "has everything," he can desire to share what he has. In fact, Kabbalah teaches that God's desire to share is the basis for all creation. God brought the world into being in order to give of himself. God can't "get" anything more than he already has. It's God's nature, therefore, to give.

In ourselves, the instinct to give and to share is genuinely god-like. This giving energy is represented by the Sefirah called Chesed. It's the desire to give what we have to others, without any resistance or restriction whatsoever on our part.

An excellent example of this desire is the relationship between parents and their newborn baby. A new parent is "hardwired" to give everything to the baby, without regard to the physical or emotional cost. If the baby cries at three o'clock in the morning, the parents automatically (or almost!) get up and provide food. If the baby needs medical attention, the parents do everything in their power to get the help that's needed, regardless of the cost. If the baby suffers any sort of injury, blaming the newborn child is obviously out of the question. The parents provide help and care with nothing held back.

The unqualified energy of giving that parents feel for a child is what the Kabbalists mean by Chesed. But that feeling is not limited to the relationship between parent and child. There are other moments in our lives when we may feel that we want nothing from another person except to give of what we have. In fact, according to Kabbalistic teaching there are even people—a very few people—who at every moment of their lives feel this way toward all living things. Abraham is said to have been such a person. He was the pure embodiment of Chesed. He wanted nothing from life except the experience of giving to others.

Once again, however, if we think about this logically, we can see some complications beginning to emerge. We have said, for example, that parents want to give everything to their newborn child. But would even the most loving mother and father give a new car to a three-month-old baby? Would they give the infant an all-expense-paid vacation to Hawaii or a state-of-the-art laptop computer? While the physical act of presenting these gifts is possible, actually doing so is absurd because the baby is not yet ready to receive and make use of what is being offered.

This is a very crucial point. It shows that the impulse toward unlimited giving has a built-in contradiction: giving is necessarily limited by the capacity of the recipient to *accept* what's being given. Parents may want their child to go to Harvard because they genuinely believe it's the best place to get a college education. But first Harvard has to accept the child, and there's a lot of homework to be done before that can happen. There'll probably even be times when the child doesn't exactly feel like doing that homework, and it may not be possible to get through that resistance without using a different energy than that of pure giving and sharing. What's more, the purpose of this is not only to have Harvard accept the child, but it's also to prepare the child so that he or she, in turn, can accept and use what Harvard has to offer.

This is where Chesed and the previous Sefirah of Gevurah must come into balance. Giving must be balanced by judgment. Sharing must be balanced by restriction. This doesn't derive from any lack of love on the part of the giver. On the contrary, it means that the giver—whether it's a parent or a teacher or even God himself—is truly committed to bringing about the greatest possible good.

—ɱ—

Every day, the world seems to tell us that happiness comes from get-
ting. But Kabbalah teaches that it is not really the world who sends
us this message. Rather, it comes from the negative side of our own
nature. God needs nothing. God lacks nothing. Therefore giving is
the essence of his nature. By making it our essence as well, we draw
closer to the unity with God that is our ultimate destiny.

God Desires the Heart

Eliezer Lippa was a simple but devout man who lived in the town of
Taranow in Poland. He wasn't well versed in Bible study and didn't
know the meaning of most of his daily prayers, but he always
prayed with the minyan, and he was scrupulous to say amen, after
every single blessing. He never conversed about worldly matters
in the synagogue, and he accorded the sages and rabbi their due
respect.

Although Eliezer Lippa knew many trades, he usually worked as
a water carrier. He worked hard and managed to make a decent
living because he had four steady customers who were well-to-do
merchants, and they paid him an above-the-average rate for his
services.

Once, the Baal Shem Tov visited Taranow. This was before his
spiritual power had been revealed to the world. He appeared to be
a simple traveler, but with a gift for telling stories. He used to con-
gregate with other laborers and tell them stories from the Bible. He
also related to them how much God was pleased by any person's
sincere prayers and straightforward faith.

One day, Eliezer Lippa was guiding his wagon with its full barrel
of water through the center of town when he spotted his friend and
fellow water carrier Zalman Dov along with some other men, gath-
ered around a ragged stranger, the Baal Shem Tov, and listening
intently to his every word.

His interest sparked, Eliezer Lippa went over to join the circle of
listeners. The Baal Shem Tov was telling the story of a wealthy man

who lived in the days when the Holy Temple in Jerusalem still stood.

"The wealthy man was taking a fattened ox to the Temple for a sacrifice. It was a massive beast, and when it decided, for reasons of its own, to stop still in its tracks, nobody was able to convince it to walk farther toward their destination. No amount of pushing could make that animal budge.

"A poor man, who was on his way home, was watching the scene. In his hand was a bunch of freshly pulled up carrots, with the green stalks still attached to the bright orange roots. Wanting to be of help to the hapless ox owner, he held the carrots to the muzzle of the ox and when it began to nibble, he pulled the carrots away and thereby led the animal to their destination at the Holy Temple.

"That night the owner of the ox had a dream. In his dream he heard a voice that called out, 'The sacrifice of the poor man, who gave up the carrots that he was bringing to his impoverished family, was a more desirable sacrifice than your fattened ox.'

"This is the lesson," said the Baal Shem Tov. "God desires the heart. Any good deed a person may perform, whether great or small, simple or difficult, is judged by the intention behind it. A deed done for God's sake, with great purity of heart, is very precious to the Creator. God cries out to the angels, 'Look at the mitzvah that has been done in my name!'"

The Creator, from his place in the heavens, saw that although the wealthy man had offered much, the poor man had offered much more.

As he listened to this story, Eliezer Lippa began to think how he longed to be able to do a mitzvah—a good deed—like the poor man in the story; with pure intention and a joyful overflowing heart. The weeks passed and still Eliezer Lippa knew no peace for the desire to be able to do such a mitzvah tortured his heart.

One day, as Eliezer Lippa was delivering water to one of his wealthy customers, he had an idea, an idea so perfect that his whole being became filled with a great sense of happiness and excitement.

Eliezer Lippa's four wealthy customers provided him with half of his livelihood since they paid him far more than the going rate for a barrel of water. On the other hand, his friend Zalman Dov supplied the town's four synagogues that paid him half the price for their water.

"I can switch four of my customers for four of his," thought Eliezer Lippa. "Four wealthy homes for four synagogues." He was anxious to serve God by providing the water in which the congregants would wash their hands. Certainly the mitzvah was of more value than the profits he would give up.

He went home and told his wife about the story of the Baal Shem Tov and how doing a mitzvah with joy is like bringing a sacrifice to the Holy Temple of ancient times. His wife readily agreed to the idea, as did Zalman Dov who sorely needed extra income. The deal was struck and the transfer of customers was made. No one but Eliezer Lippa and his wife knew what had happened, and they were overjoyed at the prospects for their new "business." There were days when even Eliezer Lippa's wife went to the river to participate in the mitzvah of drawing the water for the synagogues. Their joy was boundless. For they understood that God desires the actions of the heart.

The following story of a girl's kindness to animals is not just a sentimental greeting card. One of the unique aspects of Kabbalistic teaching is its emphasis on the obligations of human beings to all other creatures. There are many rules governing how we should treat animals, and the characters in the Bible are often revealed by how they interact with camels or sheep! Rebecca, for example, who became the wife of Isaac, is first seen offering water to all the animals in a caravan. In this way, the Bible reveals her worthiness to be the wife of a great patriarch.

Rats!

Dear Diary,

I love our new house in the suburbs! I've my own room and bathroom, but I guess most kids out here do. The park across the street doesn't even have a fence. Can you believe it? Trees everywhere. We even have a few trees of our own, and our backyard is huge, and I know I'll be the one who has to mow it. I don't really care, especially if we can get one of those mowers you can ride around on. This afternoon I sat under our jacaranda tree, which is small now but will be big soon, and according to mom, they grow very fast. Well, I'll water it. That's easy enough.

I don't miss the city, but I already miss my friends. I'm afraid we'll lose touch, even though we promised not to. School starts in two days. I'm going to be very busy, so maybe that will keep my mind off my troubles. Well, gotta go. "Dinner is served."

Dear Diary,

(It's still tonight.) So we were sitting around the dinner table, only the fourth night in our new home! Or maybe the fifth, I've kind of lost track.

Anyway, all of a sudden dad says, "I think we have rats under the house!"

Mom goes, "Please, not at the dinner table!"

But I was really interested. "Rats? How do you know we have rats, dad?"

"I heard them last night. They're nocturnal creatures."

"Nocturnal?"

"That means they come out in the dark."

"Wow, dad, you know a lot about rats!"

"I've met a few over the years."

We laughed. "Actually, I think I heard them too," I said. "You can take us away from the city, but you can't take the city away from us!"

"Well, I'll have to get some poison," Dad said.

Finally mom spoke up. "Can we please talk about something else?" So we talked about planting flowers and stuff, or at least they did. But I'm going under the house tomorrow to locate "rat central."

Dear Diary:

This morning I went to the park on my rollerblades, and there were some guys there playing softball—guys just my age. One guy was very cute. I just skated around like nothing was happening, but I was listening closely to try to find out his name. Trouble was, those guys never called each other by their names. In fact, you would not believe what they called each other. "Dawg" and stuff, like they were really in the city instead of out here in the country!

But eventually I did hear his name: Gary. Not a great name. Could be better but could be worse, but it will have to do! Anyway, I am in love with him. That was fast! Then I went home to look for the rats.

We don't really have a basement, but there's some space under the house where you can put stuff—cans of paint or whatever. Then if you go farther back, there's just dirt and a lot of wooden beams that I guess keep the house from falling down. It looked like a good place for rats, so I went to look.

And guess what! No rats—rabbits! Five baby rabbits right next to a little hole in the foundation so they can get out when they're ready. But where was mama rabbit, not to mention papa? Hiding maybe, or maybe they went to Home Depot! Anyway, I petted each one. I just couldn't resist. Maybe mama rabbit will pick up my human scent and abandon them, but if that happens I'll just feed them milk from an eyedropper. I'll take care of them. I'll raise rabbits. Why not? Also, school starts tomorrow. Wish me luck! I'm in love with Gary. It's bedtime. Sweet dreams to me!

Dear Diary:

Gary is my locker neighbor! His locker is right next to mine! I can't believe it! This was meant to be! I smiled at him, but he just gave me this blank look. Boys can be shy though. I'll say "Hi" the next time I see him.

Dear Diary:

I said "Hi" to Gary and he only nodded. Is he a snob or what? At least I met two new girls today, Taylor and Natalie. We'll all be best friends soon. We'll sit together in homeroom and have lunch together. We've already talked about Gary. They agree he's hot.

Dear Diary:

Taylor says Gary talks to her in math class. How does she get him to talk? "He started it," she says. She knows I have this huge crush on him, but I still think she's a good friend.

Tonight I told mom how I feel about Gary, and she told me not to get "boy crazy." Thanks a lot!

Dear Diary:

Oh my God! I went up to Gary in the hallway and since we're locker buddies I said, "Hi!" and he barked at me! He actually said, "Woof, woof." What does this mean? Am I

supposed to ignore this? Does he want me to keep away?
Thank God he didn't bark loud and nobody heard him.
Except me.

At dinner tonight I was still upset about the barking. But
I still told dad about going under the house and how the
rats are really rabbits. He said, "No, they're rats. Have you
ever seen baby rats? They look just like rabbits."

"And vice versa, Dad! They're rabbits. I wouldn't touch
a rat!"

"Well, maybe we can't tell what they are. But I'm not
taking any chances."

As usual, mom said, "Can we change the subject?"

"We can change it if dad doesn't kill the baby rabbits!"
So he said he'd look at them again.

But that didn't convince me. I asked mom later, in
private, to tell me when he was planning on putting out the
poison.

She said, "How would I know?"

Dear Diary:

Gary barked at me again! This time he said, "Ruff, ruff!"
Why, why, why? Before this, I dropped my books in front
of his locker, and he picked them up and gave them to me,
so I thought he could be a gentleman. I said thank you. He
said nothing. I told him I saw him playing baseball, and he
still didn't say anything. Then I asked when the next game
was and he barked at me! I ran away.

Dear Diary:

It's Saturday and today is rat poison day. So I woke up
early and dug a hole in the backyard, way in back. Then I
got a pair of rubber gloves from under the sink and went
under the house. This time the mother was there! But I

spoke to her really softly and I think she knew that I was really trying to help. Anyway, when she saw me coming, she ran over into a dark corner. So one by one I brought the babies out from under the house to the new home I had made. I carried them really close to the ground so that their mother would be able to find them. I felt kind of worried while I was doing it, but this was the only shot I had to save them. Sorry, Mrs. Rabbit, but you'll find your babies! Also, where's your husband?

Dear Diary:

It's Saturday night and I'm going to die. In the park today Taylor told me Gary is in love with her and she is in love with him. This cut like a knife. She is now my ex-best friend. I wish we had never moved here. I do not fit in. I hate this place. I hate these kids. I hate myself.

At dinner I hid my tears from my parents. Meanwhile, Dad couldn't stop talking about the "rats." He put poison under the house, so I was not allowed to go down there. Not to worry, Dad! But all of a sudden I started crying. They thought I was crying about the rats! I'm in my room with the door closed. I'm kind of surprised one of them hasn't come in here to see what's wrong but maybe they know enough to leave me alone. I don't hate them. They're just stupid.

Dear Diary:

It's Sunday morning and the most amazing thing has happened. Actually, two amazing things.

First, mom came in right before I fell asleep. She was really nice. She said, "You were upset last night about the rats?"

"Rabbits!"

"Yes, the rabbits. You were upset about them?"

"No," I said. "It's something else."

"What? Please tell me."

So I told her. "There's this boy at school that I really like a lot. And when I said hello to him, he—barked at me!

I started crying again. "Why would anybody do that?"

Mom was really calm about it. "Well, honey," she said, "he's trying to tell you that you're not pretty. 'Dog' is kind of a slang word for girls who are unattractive. So by barking, he's trying to tell you that you're a dog."

I could not believe what she was saying! She seemed so cool, calm and collected! I was almost shrieking at her. "Am I a dog? Is that what you're telling me?" I was losing it! For real!

But then she said, "No, that's definitely not what I'm telling you. I'm just explaining to you about what he was trying to say—which doesn't mean it's true. Not at all. As a matter of fact, he's being really silly. A lot of boys are at your age—"

She tried to hug me, but I did not want to hear this lecture. I started to turn away from her, but then she said, "Listen to me. I want to make you a promise. I promise you that someday soon that boy is going to want to talk with you very badly. And when he does, you just look at him and say, 'Woof, woof.'"

"Really?"

"Yes."

"When?"

"Sooner than you think. You'll be nicely surprised. So just think about that for a while."

She left. I did think about what she said. Maybe she was right, maybe not. I was looking out the window of my room, and there was my dad down below in the yard, scouting around the edge of the house. He was looking for dead rats, of course. Then something really amazing happened. Over on the other side of the yard I saw two baby rabbits just standing there in the grass. I almost jumped out of the window!

Then I tapped on the glass, and when Dad looked up, I pointed across the yard at the rabbits. I wanted to make sure that he saw them too.

—ᘓᘏ—

Chesed Summary

Of all the ten Sefirot, Chesed is most closely linked to the need for *action* in the physical world. It is not enough to read about the importance of kindness and generosity or to believe that this is the essence of God. We must act on that belief in the daily events of our lives.

But there's more. We must act with kindness and love *even when we don't feel like it*. We must give of ourselves *even to those who don't deserve it*. We must express love even when it's difficult to do so or, rather, *especially* when it's difficult.

At first glance, the idea that we should be kind and giving seems like exactly what we might expect from a spiritual or religious tradition. We're not surprised when we're told about the importance of being charitable and generous. But that's only the beginning, the easy part. Kabbalah teaches that our true purpose in life is to become one with the essence of God—*to act like God*—to the extent that acting like God is possible in the material world. To understand what that means, think about the moments in your life that you'd really like to forget: the times when you've been thoughtless, unkind, and perhaps even cruel. According to Kabbalah, God saw you in all those moments and was with you at the times that the negative and destructive side of your nature most clearly expressed itself.

Those were the moments that you were completely unlike God. Yet although you had deliberately distanced yourself from Him, God did not strike you down. There were no lightning bolts. Ten plagues were not brought down on you. Instead, God continued to extend

His love to you even though, as Kabbalah teaches, it was difficult for him to do so. God created the universe, and that was not difficult for Him, but it *is* difficult for Him to continue to love us at our worst possible moments. Yet He does so, not because we deserve it, but because the energy of Chesed is the essence of His nature.

To make this essence our own, we need to think beyond conventional acts of charity or kindness. We need to remember that God has continued to give us his love even when, by our actions, *we least deserved it*. And we must do the same for others. As we've said earlier, it isn't easy. And it isn't supposed to be easy.

CHAPTER SEVEN

Teferet

The Power of Balance

The Sefirah of Teferet expresses the principle of balance and the beauty that's created by the perfect balance of different energies. For this reason, the concept of a three-part system is very important in Kabbalah, as it is in many other spiritual traditions. At one time, for example, mathematics and especially geometry were thought of as religious traditions, and the triangle was considered especially important. A triangle's three sides and three angles give it perfect stability. It can't be collapsed or bent out of shape. You can see the importance of a three-part system in the everyday world. If you don't believe this, just try sitting on a two-legged stool!

The teachings of Kabbalah are built on three columns. The first is the Bible, or more precisely, the Bible. It is composed of five books of the Bible—Genesis, Exodus, Leviticus, Numbers, and Deuteronomy—that tell the story of Creation, the history of the people of Israel, and the laws that God gave them to live by.

The Bible, according to Kabbalah, was not composed by anyone, in the sense that an ordinary book is written down by the author. The Bible is truth in the deepest sense, and it can assume many forms. Just as human genes and chromosomes can arrange themselves to form different human bodies, the Bible can change as humanity grows and transforms—not physically, as in evolution, but spiritually, by using the tools and teachings of Kabbalah.

Before Creation, there was nothing to write the Bible on: no animal skins for making parchment, no vegetables for making papyrus, and no minerals to create slate or to make a chisel from. How was the law written? Kabbalah teaches that it was written "on the arm of God, in black fire upon white fire."

God gave the Bible that we have now to Moses, and he transmitted it to the people of Israel. But the essence of the Bible has never made its way into the world because that essence is always changing, and this is one of the most remarkable teachings of Kabbalah. It states that because what changes the Bible in the Upper World is what we do here on Earth. When we have at last fulfilled our spiritual potential and when we are finally able to receive all the love and joy that God intends for us, the Hebrew letters of the present Bible will rearrange themselves to form an entirely different document.

For example, when Adam and Eve disobeyed God in the Garden of Eden, God rearranged the letters of the Bible into words that speak of death, among other things. If the sin in the Garden had never taken place, there would have been no death, and the Bible would have been entirely different. In the same way, when the final transformation of humankind occurs, death will come to an end. There will be new spiritual laws with new meanings, although at present we cannot possibly imagine what they will be like.

The second column of Kabbalistic teachings is called the Midrash, which is essentially a commentary on the Bible. Some teachings of the Midrash were written down over the centuries, while others were only passed by word of mouth from one spiritual master to another. There was a good reason for this secrecy. This knowledge conferred powers and responsibilities on those who possessed it. Many stories make this point about the Midrash:

Once, many centuries ago, no rain fell in the land of Israel for many months. The people of the desert were used to living without much water, of course, but this was a major drought. Something had to be done.

Finally, the rabbis sent for a renowned sage known as Josef the Circle Maker, and they asked him to pray so that the rain would fall. Josef prayed, but there was no rain. Then he drew a circle, stood inside it, and asked the Creator for rain.

Josef said, "I swear by your holy name, which can never be pronounced, that I will not move until you show your children mercy."

A few drops fell. Josef then said, "Is this all that's needed? I think not!"

Suddenly a huge downpour began, and the rains fell steadily until the drought was ended.

"That's better," Josef said. "That's a real blessing."

It's easy to see how that kind of power could be dangerous, not only to the people who didn't possess it, but even to those who did. Another story about Josef the Circle Maker shows how this danger could express itself:

Josef the Circle Maker was walking along a road when he came upon a farmer planting a very unusual looking tree. "When does this tree yield fruit?" he asked.

"After seventy years," the farmer replied.

Josef asked, "And are you certain that you will even live that long?"

"My grandfather and my father planted these trees for their children," the farmer replied. "I am doing the same for mine."

Then Josef sat down under the tree and fell asleep. As darkness encircled him, he became invisible, and he slept, unseen, for seventy years. Then he awoke and saw a farmer harvesting fruit from the tree he had seen planted.

"Did you plant this tree?" Josef asked the farmer.

"No, I am the son of his son," the man answered. And Josef said to himself, "I have slept for seventy years."

Josef then returned to his own house and asked for his own son. "Josef's son is dead, but I am his son's son," a stranger told him. Then Josef went to synagogue, where he found that the rabbis quoted him as a great Kabbalist. They dispensed wisdom in the name of Josef the Circle Maker. But when Josef told the scholars, "I am he," no one believed him. So Josef wept, and died. All this came about because he had made himself invisible.

The third pillar of Kabbalah is the secret interpretations of the Bible, as expressed in the Zohar and the other writings of the Kabbalistic masters. This is the true soul of the law, which for thousands of years was revealed only to the chosen few. Much of it has been hidden until now, and finally the wisdom is being revealed. But no matter how much of the Kabbalah is known, there will always be more that remains undisclosed.

It is said that when Adam was in the Garden of Eden, the Creator sent him a book by the hand of the angel Raphael, the custodian of holy mysteries. In this book were inscriptions from the original Bible and 72 kinds of wisdom, which themselves became 670 infinite mysteries. In the middle of this book, Adam found an inscription that revealed the 1500 keys that were withheld even from the angels and hidden in this book meant for Adam alone.

That book was with Adam from the beginning, until he went out from the Garden of Eden and into the world. Before he sinned, Adam studied that book and learned from it secrets unknown even to the angels. But after he had transgressed and eaten of the fruit of the tree of knowledge of good and evil, that book flew away, his body began to get smaller, and his splendor dimmed.

In that moment, the Creator in his mercy had the angel Raphael return the book to Adam. And Adam bequeathed this book to his son Seth, and Seth passed it down through his descendants until the book reached Abraham. From this book, Abraham learned to behold the glory of the Creator. But there was much more that was not in the book or in any book that has ever come into the world:

The Kabbalist Hayyim Vital once asked his teacher, Rabbi Isaac Luria about the meaning of a passage in the Zohar, which concealed a great mystery. Rabbi Isaac Luria replied, "For your sake and for my sake and for the sake of the whole world, I will not unfold this thing to you, Rabbi Hayyim Vital, for there's a great mystery here that those in heaven do not want revealed."

"But you must!" said Rabbi Hayyim Vital.

"If I do this thing," said Rabbi Isaac Luria, "I warn you that, as much as you desire to hear it now, you will regret hearing it a thousand times more. But I am required to answer your every question, so please do not require this of me."

"Nevertheless, explain," said Rabbi Hayyim Vital.

So Rabbi Isaac Luria opened these secrets and then informed his student that even as the gates were opened, a decree was passed in heaven that he, Rabbi Isaac Luria, would die that very year, as a punishment for having revealed these secrets.

"And furthermore," the teacher explained, "you have brought this misfortune on your head, for had you not pressed me, I would have not revealed it. And even though I hinted at misfortune, you did not heed my warning."

And what did he reveal? We still do not know, for it is buried in the heart of Rabbi Hayyim Vital, and he will not reveal it until he and Rabbi Isaac Luria and everyone who ever lived is reborn, at the transformation of the world.

Stories like these teach us that the balance of spiritual wisdom depends as much on those who teach and those who learn as on the content of the teachings themselves. Through the condition of our own souls, we determine what teachings can be brought into the world and even what the teachings consist of in the world above.

Like many Kabbalistic teachings, this is a difficult concept to make clear, but it can be explained very easily through a children's game. One player thinks of a word, and the second player is allowed to ask twenty questions in order to determine what the word might be. This is a very old game, and the traditional first question is, "Are you thinking of an animal, a vegetable, or a mineral?" In other words, is the secret a person, a pet, a plant, or a form of rock? From this point on, each question can become more and more sharply focused, until finally the secret can be identified.

This is a fun game, but it's not the one that reveals the truth about Kabbalah. For that, we need to look at another variation. The game proceeds just as before, except this time no secret word is required when the game begins. The word is created by the questions that are asked. Until you are asked, "Is it animal, vegetable, or mineral?" you have not made that decision. You make it when the question is asked, and not before. In this way, the questioner creates the answer instead of just looking for it.

This is exactly what we do at every moment of our lives. We think we are looking for the answer, but we are actually bringing the answer into being by the very nature of our search. If our consciousness is out of balance in one direction or another, the answer that we find—and the world that we live in—will always reflect that fact.

When you feel that you are becoming either too easygoing or too demanding of others, be aware that these are the energies of Chesed and Gevurah asserting themselves in your life. Then connect with Teferet, the Sefirah of balance. If you do this, you will not only bring about internal change but you will also change the world around you, not just how you perceive the world, but what it actually is. This is an essential precept of Kabbalah.

The previous two Sefirot, Gevurah and Chesed, are highly emotional. Their energy is that of the heart more than the mind. Teferet is a more rational connection. Yet Kabbalah teaches that the person who has demonstrated the balance and restraint throughout life that define Teferet can also attain mystical powers, as the following story describes.

The Grandfather

Rabbi Aryeh Leib was known as "Grandfather," since he emulated the ways of our ancestor Abraham the patriarch. His home was always open to guests, and he loved his fellow human beings with a genuine and all-encompassing love. In fact, within a short time after he arrived in any town, every Jew there became a dedicated and pious individual.

The Grandfather had a student of Kabbalah who was very devoted. The student's name was Jacob, and he was actually quite a wealthy businessman. But Jacob had been married for many years and still had not been blessed with children. On numerous occasions he came to beseech his rabbi for a blessing that would help him gain a family, yet the Grandfather rejected his request every time.

One day, Jacob and his wife decided that enough was enough. They made a decision that he would go to beseech the rabbi once more. This time he resolved that no matter what, he would not take no for an answer.

Jacob found the rabbi absorbed in a private study. He interrupted the rabbi gently and told him the reason for his appearance. The Grandfather told him that he was involved in a matter of great importance having to do with the welfare of the world, and now was not the time to accept individual petitions.

When Jacob realized that the rabbi might actually be speaking to the Almighty face to face, he understood that this was an auspicious moment, and he redoubled his efforts to gain a blessing from the Grandfather. He was so relentless that finally, with more than a trace of aggravation in his voice, the Grandfather turned on Jacob with the full force of his presence and assured him that he would never merit having a child.

Broken and distressed over his tragic mistake, the man went on his way. If there was even a minute chance that he might have a child before, there was certainly no chance now. He absorbed himself in his business and his travel to forget his anguish.

One day he came to the town of Koretz, where there lived another famous Kabbalist known as Rabbi Pinchas. Jacob had spent enough time around the Grandfather to recognize a person of exemplary qualities when he saw one. He decided to get to know Rabbi Pinchas, in the hope that maybe one day Rabbi Pinchas could reverse the curse of the Grandfather. Therefore Jacob made a point of visiting Koretz as often as possible.

Once, he arrived in Koretz a few days before Passover. Rabbi Pinchas was sitting in the synagogue learning and praying and, as usual, was living in total poverty. Nevertheless, even the approaching holiday did not cause him to waver from his studies.

Jacob went to Rabbi Pinchas's wife and inquired whether they had the means with which to celebrate the upcoming Passover. The wife informed him that they had neither meat nor chicken nor fish nor wine nor candles nor even the unleavened bread called matzoh and no prospects were in sight for obtaining any of these things.

Then Jacob told the wife, "I will provide everything for the entire holiday if you will let me be at the Seder." The wife readily agreed.

When Rabbi Pinchas left his house the morning before Passover, he knew that there were none of the provisions needed for the holiday. He went to his studies as on any other day.

As soon as Rabbi Pinchas left, Jacob and the rabbi's wife went to work. The previously ordered supplies began to arrive. When darkness fell over Koretz and the candles were lit, the home of Rabbi Pinchas was prepared for royalty. There were meat and fish and chicken. There was matzoh, and there were wines of every type. Fresh fruits from all over the world were piled high in baskets. All the furniture in the house was replaced. The table was decked with a new snowy-white cloth and a tall candelabrum, as well as new porcelain dishes, gleaming silverware, and golden cups. The children and the rabbi's wife had new outfits, and a white silk cloth was draped over the back of Rabbi Pinchas's chair.

The family anxiously awaited the arrival of Rabbi Pinchas. But he, knowing that there was nothing to come home to, stayed on at the synagogue for a while after prayer before he finally turned for home. When he walked in the door and saw all that was before him, he was speechless. He immediately and with great exultation began to bless the wine and to recite the Passover service. Rabbi Pinchas's exuberance was infectious, and the family sang and chanted and discussed the Exodus from Egypt with great passion until it was time for the Seder meal.

It was then that Rabbi Pinchas turned to his wife and asked for an explanation of how all of this had happened. She motioned to the guest indicating that he had wanted to spend Passover with them and provided the bounty.

Rabbi Pinchas, still in a rapturous state, turned to the guest and asked him whether there was anything that he could do for him. Jacob, realizing that his chance at last had come, broke down and told the whole story of how he'd been a student of the Grandfather and how he and his wife had been childless for so many years. He then explained how he never merited a blessing from his rabbi until he bothered him when he shouldn't have and thus received a curse instead of a blessing.

Rabbi Pinchas, being in the exalted state that he was and very moved by the man's story replied, "If I have any influence in the Heavens at all, it is my oath that this year you will be blessed with a child!"

At the moment that Rabbi Pinchas made his oath, a great tumult erupted in the Heavens. Here were two promises, made by two great rabbis, and they contradicted each other. Whose would be upheld? The Heavenly Court finally decided to examine the chronicles of the lives of each rabbi. They found that only Rabbi Pinchas had been so careful in his speech that he had never made an unqualified promise or oath. Therefore, Jacob and his wife were indeed blessed with a child within the year. And the renown of Rabbi Pinchas began to spread.

—ɱ—

A corral in Arizona may seem like an unlikely setting for Kabbalistic insights about Teferet. But the young girl in this story learns a lesson about keeping your balance, both physically and spiritually.

Rodeo Runaway

Lydia was born in a large city in the northeastern United States, and her family lived there until she was five years old. Then, for reasons that were very difficult for her to understand, her father decided it would be best if the family moved over two thousand miles away, to a remote corner of southern Arizona near the New Mexico border.

Although it was a long time ago, Lydia remembered listening to her parents talking about the decision to move to Arizona. It was late at night. She and her sister Beth had sneaked out of their bedroom and hid near the dining room door where their parents were talking. Lydia's father wanted to move because he thought they could have a lot more space for a lot less money. Lydia's mother seemed to understand that, but she was worried about leaving her friends and her job.

She seemed to feel really bad about leaving her job, which was difficult for Lydia to understand. Why would anyone want to have a job? Then her father said that when they moved to Arizona they could save so much money that Lydia's mom wouldn't even need to work anymore. This made sense, but her mother was still upset. She actually started to cry about it, and that was when Lydia knew they really were going to leave. Crying is always a last resort, and it almost never works.

Sitting there on the floor in the darkness, Lydia knew that she and Beth were thinking the same thing. They were looking around into the living room, where the shapes of the sofa, the chairs, and the television set were barely visible. They knew that before too long they would be in a different kind of home in a very new environment. The same furniture might be there with them, but it would look different. They might also be the same people, but they would look different to each other and to themselves. Lydia really did not know much about Arizona. Whatever it was, she knew she would just have to get used to it.

For the first five years of her life, Lydia had been trying to learn how to get along with people. For the next ten years, starting when she arrived in Arizona, she learned about getting along with animals—cows, horses, and even coyotes. One of her earliest memories of her new home was falling off a horse. It's not really that far to the ground, but it happens so unexpectedly that you usually land really hard. You have to learn that and be ready for it. You also have to learn to get back onto the horse right away. It's not easy to learn either of those things, but they're both important.

Lydia's father worked for the Arizona Department of Agriculture. When the family lived in the northeast, he worked for the federal government, sitting behind a desk and reading reports about what was happening on farms and ranches around the country. Now he was happy because he could drive around and see what was happening with his own eyes. In fact, he could see it even without driving around because now he had a small ranch of his own.

It was exciting and different from the city. Before, Beth and Lydia had gotten excited about riding around the block on their bicycles. Now that seemed so tame, because each one of them had their own horse to ride! Their father got them the horses after they'd been in Arizona for only a few weeks. It had taken them years to get bicycles, and now they had horses in almost no time at all. They could tell their dad was really happy being out of the city, and as soon as Lydia got the horse, she was happy too.

For many weeks to come, while the kids back east were going out to the movies, Lydia was learning to put a bridle and saddle on her very own horse. Beth had one too, of course, but Lydia's was much more interesting—or so it seemed to her. He was a five-year-old white horse named Apache. He certainly wasn't the biggest or the fastest or the most beautiful horse she had seen since coming to Arizona. But Lydia knew that his ancestors actually belonged to cowboys and Indians, and that made him a really amazing horse.

There were some other interesting things about Apache too. Horses are not the brightest animals, but Lydia thought they did have a kind of sly sense of humor. Or maybe she was just trying to look at the bright side of things, since there was a possibility that some of the things horses did weren't intended to be funny. For example, it wasn't a good idea to go riding wearing anything other than cowboy boots. The toes of those boots are very hard, and there's a good reason for that. If a horse sees a chance to step on your toe while you're trying to bridle or saddle him, he'll usually go for it—and you'll be sorry that you chose to go riding in your tennis shoes.

For the same reason—and again, maybe they're just trying to be funny—horses have a really good eye for trees that are close enough together so that the horse can pass between them but not the rider on his back. You might think that this situation doesn't come up very often, but it does happen occasionally. Lydia was galloping along with Apache one time, and he must've noticed a pair of trees that were just the right distance apart. He ran straight toward them, and there was nothing for her to do but to hop up onto the saddle with both her feet and somehow try to hold on until they'd passed through the trees. What a good trick! (Apache was also really good at spotting low-hanging branches.)

But the most exciting experience Lydia had with Apache didn't take place out on the trail. Instead, it happened at a corral she had visited to audition for a kids' rodeo. In order to be in the rodeo, you had to have your own horse, and you had to show that you could ride well. For kids, there wouldn't be any real rodeo stuff, like calf roping or bull riding, but there would be a short race in which you had to guide your horse around some obstacles. So the organizers wanted to make sure that everybody knew how to ride.

Their father took Beth and Lydia to the tryout. They were in their truck, with the horses in a trailer behind. Their father had decided they should arrive a little late. He was sure that there would be many other kids, and he didn't see any point in having to stand around waiting. But as it turned out, there weren't many kids at all. By the time they arrived, nobody else was there except the two guys who were in charge of the rodeo, so Beth and Lydia didn't have to wait at all.

Beth went first. She took her horse out of the trailer, put a saddle and bridle on him, and rode him around the track that circled the corral. When she came back, the two guys said that Beth had done fine, and she would be able to participate in the event. Then it was Lydia's turn. With her dad's help, she got Apache out of the trailer. Then came the bridle, the saddle blanket, and finally the saddle, which was so heavy she couldn't do it herself, but she wasn't really expected to. Then she headed through the corral gate onto the track.

Sometimes Lydia really felt she could tell what mood her horse was in, but at that time she wasn't as tuned in as she later became. In those first months after she arrived in Arizona, she probably projected her own mood onto the horse—and on that particular day she was feeling really good. It was a beautiful morning, the mountains looked great against the clear blue sky, and she was really excited about being in the rodeo. Apache was trotting nicely around the track, and she thought it might be fun to try something a bit more adventurous. So she touched him with her boot heels and made the little clicking sound she used when she wanted him to run. She certainly wasn't nervous because there wasn't much that could go wrong. She had never been thrown from a horse, and there were no trees that he could run between. There weren't even any low branches.

So they started to go. Apache was able to run fast when he wanted to, and on that day he wanted to. Lydia was amazed at how quickly they made that first lap around the track. It was as if they were flying! She could see her father watching, along with Beth and the two rodeo guys. They looked impressed, as if Lydia were giving a famous racehorse his morning workout. The only problem was, Apache showed no interest in slowing down as they came to the end of the first lap. They blew past the gate and kept right on going around the track.

By this time Lydia was leaning forward in the saddle in order to keep her balance, and she was holding the reins close behind the back of the horse's neck. In Western-style riding, both reins are held in the left hand, and she was using her right hand to hold on to Apache's mane. When she tried to pull back on the reins, it was like trying to pull a car out of a ditch with your bare hands. It had absolutely no effect. The horse weighed at least ten times more than she did, so who was she kidding? Certainly not Apache!

As they passed the gate for the second time, Lydia could see that the onlookers had somewhat different expressions on their faces. Her dad in particular looked a bit puzzled and maybe a little concerned. But there was one thing Lydia knew for sure: she wasn't going to ask for help. She wasn't going to start waving her arms and crying. She was just going to keep going, because she really didn't see any way to stop.

Lydia wasn't sure how many more times they went around—probably not more than two or three. But it was one of those weird experiences in which time seemed to slow down, like what sometimes happens when there's a car accident in a movie. In fact, even though she was holding on for dear life as the horse raced around the track, she realized she wasn't really frightened. She knew she should have been frightened, but as they kept going she somehow started to get used to it. Now she felt excited, but strangely safe at the same time.

She had been looking at the sky and the mountains when they first started, but now she became aware of the scent of the horse's mane, the texture of the leather rein in her hand, and the sound of hooves pounding rhythmically on the ground. Most noticeable of all was Apache's breathing as he ran. He was really trying as hard as he could.

"Why is he doing this?" Lydia wondered. "What could he be trying to prove?"

It's hard to explain how being carried around by a runaway horse can be a time for insight and reflection, but that truly is what happened. Somehow Lydia understood that there were really two very different kinds of beings interacting at that moment. One of them was probably a lot smarter than the other one was, at least in the way people measure intelligence. But the other one was much, much stronger. Maybe it was even smarter in some ways. It certainly knew more about horses!

Strange as it seems, this led Lydia to some deep insights or at least they seemed deep to her. It was as if what was happening between her and the horse was the same thing that was happening all the time between people and God. There's just a tremendous gap in the ability of one to understand the other. She realized that God is supposed to know everything, but sometimes it must seem to him that we're just running wild. Meanwhile, we can't understand how God can allow all the terrible things that are taking place. Yet we're stuck with each other. We just have to see where it all leads us and hope that something really bad doesn't happen along the way.

But the main thing that she realized that day was that there is absolutely no point in fighting against something that not only is more powerful than you are, but also seems to be operating from such a different point of view. If she had really fought against Apache that day, there was an excellent chance she would have been hurt—not really by him, but by her own misguided response to the situation. Instead, she had the good sense just to let things "run their course." After all, even if she didn't try to stop him, it was hard to imagine that Apache would keep running for very long. If she just used a little trust and restraint, he was certain to stop by himself after a few laps around the track.

That's exactly what happened. Finally, Apache got tired and started to slow down. Whether he was physically tired or just tired of another joke he was playing on a young girl was very hard to say. But in the end, he was just huffing and puffing and snorting as they walked through the gate and back toward the waiting onlookers.

By this time, they definitely looked concerned, but Lydia had a bright smile on her face. "That was great!" she said, patting Apache on his sweaty neck. "I hope I didn't keep you waiting. I just wanted to show you how fast he could run!"

Today Lydia doesn't even remember what happened at the rodeo. She still has Apache, but both of them are quite a bit older now. He doesn't have the mischievous impulses that he used to have. But whenever she's around him—and she's around him a lot—she always remembers the lesson she learned that day on the track. When you're facing something that's much bigger and stronger than you are, better to trust that a good outcome will happen than to fight against what's happening.

That doesn't mean you can just stop trying. You still have to hold on and you can't just let go of the reins. But if you focus on controlling yourself instead of struggling against forces that are beyond your control, you can enjoy the ride. You can even turn it into the ride of your life.

—《〜—

Teferet Interpretation

We've seen that the number three is a foundation of strength and stability throughout nature. The triangle, for example, is an extremely durable form that is used in all sorts of structures, both natural and synthetic. In Kabbalah too, the Sefirot are divided into

three columns, with the middle column bringing balance and har-
mony into the space between the other two.

The Sefirah of Teferet is especially important in this respect, since
it balances two energies that are always at work in our everyday
lives. These are Chesed, which is the inclination toward kindness
and generosity, and Gevurah, which expresses the power of judgment. Teferet is the mediator between these two poles. It's the resolution of two extremes, both of which are supremely important but
which need to be balanced in order for our lives to be truly fulfilled.

Suppose, for example, that you're just learning how to drive a
car. If you get behind the wheel of a car that has not been equipped
with brakes, you're going to have some real problems. You may be
able to get where you want to go, but you won't be able to stop
when you arrive there—unless you crash into the wall! On the other
hand, you may be safer in a car that has brakes and no gas pedal,
but you'll never be able to get out of the parking lot. Instead, you
need the complete package: the framework that makes both speed-
ing up and slowing down possible, but in ways that are appropriate
to the needs of the moment. This is exactly what the balancing
energy of Teferet accomplishes.

The metaphor of a courtroom is also very useful for understanding Teferet. When a trial is in progress, both the prosecuting attorney and the attorney for the defense have very one-sided roles. The
prosecutor tries to show the defendant in the most negative possible
light, while the defendant's lawyer tries to depict his client as a completely innocent human being. The judge, however, must mediate
between these two points of view, and the instrument of this media-
tion is the law itself. The law allows certain kinds of behavior from
both the prosecution and the defense, while other behaviors are
excluded. Out of this comes justice—a middle ground between
unadulterated judgment and complete acceptance and mercy.

The ancient Kabbalists viewed the biblical character of Jacob as
the embodiment of this form of spiritual energy. Jacob was the third

of the great patriarchs. He was the grandson of Abraham, who was the perfect embodiment of kindness and gentleness, and he was the son of Isaac, who represented the power of judgment. Jacob had elements of both his father and his grandfather; as a result, he is a complete person, able to call on a range of responses as the situation demands. There are times when Jacob is very gentle. When Rachel and Leah trick him into marrying the "wrong" sister, he does indeed get angry, but then he agrees to work another seven years for Laban in order to marry the woman he loves. Yet he is also capable of fighting fiercely—and winning—in a night-long wrestling contest against a supernatural being.

Understanding the importance of Teferet can be immensely helpful in your life, but it requires the ability to get outside the emotions of the moment in order to see the situation objectively. When you feel hurt, insulted, or wronged, your first impulse will likely be to strike back at the person who has done this to you: to take "justice" into your own hands. But you may also encounter people who know how to take advantage of you without your even realizing it. They may be so good at tapping into your kindly inclinations that your powers of insight and judgment are completely disabled. When you feel yourself being pulled very strongly in one direction or another, make a conscious effort toward connecting with the balancing energy of Teferet. It's rarely easy to do, and sometimes it's not even easy to realize that it needs to be done, but the ability to steer a middle course is essential for enjoying your life to the fullest.

CHAPTER EIGHT

Binah

The Power of Knowledge

B inah is the power to know how things work in the world, which includes the workings of your own heart. It is not the highest realm of understanding—it is not wisdom—but it is the gateway to that realm. We can achieve the knowledge that Binah represents through our own efforts, both in study and in action. When we sincerely devote ourselves to gaining that knowledge, perhaps for many years, wisdom will come to us by itself.

Some people study Kabbalah because they want things to be different in their lives, and then they fall into doubt if they do not receive what they want. They defeat themselves by continually feeling that they are not getting what they deserve. But there is a reason for everything that happens in the universe. Sometimes it is not yet your time to receive.

There was a man who had—for twenty-five years, every day—prayed to receive one million dollars in his bank account. Yet he did not receive one million dollars. Finally, he complained to the rabbi, saying,"Rabbi, my prayers are not being heard. My prayers are not being answered." The rabbi looked at him with surprise. "Yes, your prayers are being heard. They are being answered. The answer is no."

This world was meant to give us what we need, which is not necessarily always identical to what we want. The most famous Kabbalists cautioned that modesty, the realization that we live within limits, is the mark of a good teacher.

Regarding this, the sixteenth-century Kabbalist Moses Cordovero suggested that we "try to learn from someone who has followed paths of integrity as far as possible." He also counseled to exercise patience: "Even if it seems that you do not understand, do not stop, because God will faithfully help you discover hidden wisdom. . . . If something in this wisdom seems doubtful to you, wait. . . . Those who persevere in this wisdom find that when they ponder these teachings many times, knowledge grows within them."

There are no shortcuts in Kabbalah. We have to do the work. But for the same reason, Kabbalistic meditation is not about learning how to cope. As we develop as human beings and perform more and more positive actions, we are able to remove many of the obstacles that limit the amount of God's Light that is available to us. We are able to ask for more—and this is good—to ask for the most from life, to vanquish what keeps us from achieving our goals, and to live truly in freedom. Problems that are with us in our lives will keep on repeating themselves until they are removed. Kabbalah is not a way to escape our problems, but instead it helps us to take responsibility for our lives, to confront our problems, to go right into the eye of the hurricane, and to be so strong that we can hold our ground.

This story is from the eighteenth chapter of the biblical book of Genesis. By this time, the patriarch Abraham was almost a hundred years old. Long ago God had promised him that he would be the father of the Jewish people, yet Abraham and his wife Sarah still did not have a child. Yet Abraham had gained a great deal of knowledge in his long life. He had learned to be always ready to serve God, especially when he least expected it.

The Three Strangers

Long ago, in the time of Abraham and Sarah, a very hot day dawned on the ancient land of Canaan. God had opened a hole in the earth so that the heat of hell escaped into the air, bringing about the hottest day in the history of the world.

No one was more miserable than Abraham was, the great patriarch of the Jewish people. But it wasn't the heat itself that made him uncomfortable. He was uncomfortable because there were no travelers on the road to whom Abraham could give food and drink. Abraham was one of those rare people whose purpose in life was to help others. Nothing made him happier than sharing his hospitality with strangers. But now, because of the heat, no one at all was on the road.

Despite his age—he was almost a hundred years old—Abraham even went out and looked for people who might be incapacitated by the heat. But there was nobody to be found. So while his wife Sarah remained inside the tent, Abraham sat in the doorway and closed his eyes in prayer.

Then something very strange and surprising happened. Abraham looked up for a moment, and there were three men coming toward him across the sand. How could this be possible? Just a few seconds before there had been nobody for miles around, and now these men were already quite nearby. Abruptly, Abraham broke off his prayer. He hoped that God would forgive him, but he considered the duty of hospitality to be even more important than speaking with the Lord.

Abraham quickly suspected that there was something very powerful and mysterious about the strangers who had so suddenly appeared. His suspicions were confirmed by a magical tree that grew near his tent. Whenever a righteous person came near the tree, it spread out its branches to offer shade. But in the presence of an evil person, the trees branches turned upward so that they cast no shade. As the three strangers passed nearby, the tree spread its branches wider than ever before. Now Abraham knew that these were holy beings. In fact, he believed they were angels—and that is exactly what they were. Their names were Michael, Raphael, and Gabriel.

Abraham immediately offered them food and drink, just as he would have offered to any other visitors. But in this case he made a bit more of an effort than usual. He hurriedly slaughtered a cow and prepared its meat, and he directed his wife to bake three loaves of fine bread, one for each of the visitors. But Sarah, for her part, was not quite sure what all the fuss was about. Like her husband, she was a spiritual being of the highest rank. But being childless had caused her great emotional pain, and as a result she had lost touch with some of her power. Although Abraham immediately recognized the visitors' supernatural identity, Sarah did not see this.

When the food was ready, Abraham placed it before the guests. The three angels thanked their host, and it appeared to Abraham that they had eaten. But angels don't need food the way human beings do. They may look like they have physical bodies, but they really don't. So they did not eat anything that Abraham put before them, but it appeared to Abraham that they did. Instead, they used a divine fire to cause the food to disappear.

When the meal was completed, Michael, who was the greatest of the angels, thanked Abraham for being such a gracious host. Then he got to his feet and drew a line on the wall of the tent. "When the first rays of the sun strike this line, Sarah will have conceived a child," he said. Then he drew another line. "And when the time of year comes in which the sun's first rays strike here, Sarah will give birth to a son."

As this was going on, Sarah was listening from inside the tent. She heard what the visitor said, and she could not keep herself from laughing. "How can I possibly believe that I will become the mother of a child? My body is old and shriveled! And how I can ever believe that Abraham will become a father? He's even older than I am!"

Then God spoke to Sarah: "Why did you laugh?"

"I didn't," Sarah protested, like a child who has been caught doing something very wrong.

"Yes, you did laugh," God told her, just like a parent. "Do you doubt my wisdom? Do you doubt that I can see the future in the present?"

Then he spoke to Abraham. "Sarah doubts the word of my angels. She believes she is too old to give birth to a son. But am I too old to bring forth miracles?"

It's important to note that God told Abraham only part of what Sarah said. God referred to Sarah's doubts about her own ability to bear children, but he did not repeat what she said about Abraham's age. There was a very down-to-earth reason for this. Even for God, telling something other than the "whole" truth is justified in order to prevent ill feeling between a husband and a wife. One year later Sarah gave birth to Isaac.

—ɯ—

It's a big jump from the desert of thousands of years ago to a modern high school classroom. But the boy in this story discovers a lesson similar to what Sarah had to learn: you must know that if you have a destiny that is to be fulfilled, it will happen—and probably in a way that you never expected.

Paperback Writer

"Put down that Game Boy! Pay attention please!"

That was my English teacher, and he was looking straight at me. His name is Mr. Ferdinand, but we all called him Ferdy or sometimes Ferdinand the Bull. He's not really a bad guy. It's not his fault he's a dufus. Anyway, I put my Game Boy down, but I didn't turn it off. And he just kept talking.

"People, book reports are coming due. If you haven't started writing, you'd better get going. If you haven't started reading, you'd better get the next train out of town."

I couldn't wait for school to be over. Not just for that day, but forever. Mostly, when I wasn't playing with my Game Boy, I just philosophized about the nature of time. Why couldn't it move any faster? Half an hour to go. Tick tock, tick tock. Fifteen minutes. Ten. *Ring!*

Finally! The whole class stood up and stretched. It had been a long pull. I turned to my bud Brendan and smiled. "Another month and I'm outta here, Bren!"

"Yeah. And then what?"

"Harvard!"

We both laughed and high fived, and I hurried on over to the comic store. I do like to read! I just don't like to read books. In fact, I'll read almost anything else—ads, labels, graffiti, and license plates. But comics are my favorite. I've been reading them since I was a kid, and I'm still a kid at heart. Comics keep you young!

Back at home, I was into my third *Spiderman* when mom walked in. The first words out of her mouth were, "Do you have any homework?"

"I don't think so."

"Think again."

"Okay." So I thought again and then went back to my room.

It always made me feel good to walk in and see all the cardboard boxes filled with my comics collection. Hundreds of them! The collection was my secret weapon. Someday it would be worth a lot of money. Maybe it already was! After graduation, I'd get some more comics and then sell all of them to a serious collector and have enough for a down payment on a condo.

Later, I'd do dinner with mom, have a polite conversation talking about nothing much. My parents are divorced. Dad is in Argentina shooting a documentary about some kind of animal. Or maybe it's a bird. Definitely not a fish. It was a typical night at home. Pretty much all of them were the same.

A week went by. I was back in Ferdy's English class. "So, people, you have four days until that book report is due." Then the bell rang.

I looked at Brendan. "What book report?"

"The book report, dude! I read an easy one somebody gave me. About a lamb."

"I better get one too."

"Maybe so! Okay, see ya!"

Nothing too memorable happened for a while. One night my dad e-mailed me some photos, and I dreamed about playing basketball in the Andes. The air was so thin that I kept hitting three pointers. Pretty nice dream. But at school the next day, I walked into Ferdy's class and totally freaked when I saw what was written on the blackboard: Book Reports Now Due.

"Brendan! Did you know about this?"

"Sure, man. We even talked about it."

"But I don't have a book report. What am I going to do now?"

"Hey, don't stress. You'll think of something."

Just then Ferdy walked in. The first thing he said was, "Okay, everybody pass the book reports up to the front of the room." But he seemed to be staring right at me. I took out a blank sheet of paper and passed it forward.

At the front of the room, Ferdy was looking through all the reports. He stopped at the blank paper and asked, "Whose is this?"

"Mr. Ferdinand, I cannot tell a lie. It's mine. I forgot my book report at home today."

"Is it done?"

I looked offended. "Yes! Certainly!"

His face was red. "Well, why didn't you bring it? You'd forget your head if it wasn't attached to your neck!"

"I swear I'll bring it in tomorrow. I can even go home right now and get it," I bluffed.

"No, just bring it tomorrow," he said, "and if you don't, I'll fail you!" Wow. Wow. This man took his job very seriously. I guess he wanted us to do the same thing. Slowly his face returned to a normal color, and he began his usual drone. I spaced out for the rest of the class. As hard as I tried to think about my comics or basketball, I just couldn't concentrate. The book report kept popping into my mind.

I went home. Mom was working late. Like a maniac, I scoured the house for books. Mom had some romance novels, but I could tell they weren't Ferdy's cup of nonfat latte. I sat down on my bed and tried to think. What had I read? Actually, it seemed like I'd read a lot. Just no books. Why couldn't I think of anything? Was I stupid? As they say in the comics, "No, no!"

Then something came over me. I went to my desk and sat in the chair. I opened the drawer and took out a piece of paper. I started writing. Me! Writing!

Title: Bitter Fruit.
Author: Jose Lopez

The plot of this book is very interesting. There was this amazing girl in the Andes Mountains. Her name was Angela, a rare beauty with emerald green eyes. Since early childhood, she was also a great athlete. She could outrun any kid up the highest hill. She could run faster and jump faster than any of them could. One day, an NBA scout from America, Pete Monroe, was on vacation in her village and met her. She had a ball, but not a basketball. But it bounced anyway. Her father made a hoop based on directions from Pete Monroe. Pete saw that Angela was a genius basketball player. He had to take her back to the United States with him. He gave her father a check for five million dollars.

Up in New York City, Angela was afraid of the strange environment. She stayed with Pete and his family. He became like a father to Angela. She looked up to him.

Angela learned the game quickly and was soon the star of
the New York Knicks. She was the only woman who had
ever played in the NBA. Angela was going to be famous.
But there was one problem. Now she was in love with Pete
and Pete was happily married. Angela told Pete that she
wanted him to leave his wife. She couldn't live without
him. He was her first love. He told her she'd find another
one, and that first loves are like bitter fruit.

Dazed and confused, Angela ran away. She got lost in
New York City. While wandering about she noticed the
fruit stands. She did not like what Pete had told her, so she
cried. She hadn't cried since she was a baby. These were
bitter tears, she thought. Pete would never understand, but
in her village, when a woman gives herself to a man, he
must take care of her and love and marry her.

Meanwhile, Pete looked high and low for Angela in
every hospital and other institutions. He filed a missing
person's report, and she was all over the news. But Angela
didn't want to be found. Once someone said they saw her
on the Brooklyn Bridge. Then someone said they spotted
her looking down from the rooftop of a building. Some
think that she flew back home. Pete went crazy with guilt.
Pete realized he didn't want to live without her and would
find her one day.

Many years later, his wife handed him a note. It was
written by Angela years before. His wife was jealous of her
and never gave him the note, but she finally did. It said,
"My dear love, where I come from, we don't have bitter
fruit." And Pete sat down and cried. The End.

Finished! I read it over and over. It seemed like a real book. I'd tell
Ferdy my dad got it in South America. An English translation. They
didn't publish it here. That would work! The next day, I handed in
my book report. I forgot about it, but it didn't forget about me. On
Friday Ferdy called me into his office to discuss my report.

"This Pete Monroe, is he fictional or real?"

"Oh, he's fictional. At least I think so!"

"Fascinating. What a great story! So touching!"

"You really liked it?"

"Yes. It seems like a good book, and you did a nice job on the report."

"Really? Thanks, Mr. Ferdinand. Have a great day!"

I turned and started out of the office. But then he said, "You know, I'd love to see that book."

"Oh—Well, unfortunately I don't have it anymore."

"You don't have it anymore? What happened to it? Did the dog eat it?"

"No! Ha ha!"

"Well, what did you do with it then?"

Uh oh, his face was starting to get red. Did he smell a rat? I had to think fast.

"Well, what happened was this. I was walking across a bridge the other day, on my way to school. I thought of Angela in the story. Was this story true? Would she have jumped off the Brooklyn Bridge? I looked into the dark greenish water and imagined what it would be like to jump. The book was in my hand, as I stared into the river far below—"

"It fell in?"

"No! It didn't!"

Why didn't I just say it fell in? Why couldn't I take the easy way out? Because I was on a roll, that's why!

"I held on tight to the book. Then, after school, I went to Chinatown. Maybe Angela went there when she ran away. So I went to the tallest building in Chinatown. I found the stairs, went to the roof, and looked out over the city. As I looked down at the people below, I felt like I was in Tibet—or the Andes! Then I saw a girl who fit Angela's description. I yelled down to her, but she didn't hear me. So, I dropped the book so it would land a few steps in front of her, but it landed behind her instead. A man picked it up. He looked up and saw me. I yelled at him, "Stop that girl!" He nodded. I don't know if he spoke English because he was Chinese. But he went into a shop a few doors down. I ran back into the building and flew down the steps. When I reached the street, I ran in her direction. But she was gone, He was gone. And my book was gone."

Ferdy shook his head."Fascinating!"

"Fascinating? Again?"

"If it wasn't true, it would make great fiction."

"Thanks, Mr. Ferdinand!"

"Thank you. I'll look for that book on the Internet. It's got to be somewhere."

"Yes, I'm sure you're right."

I started to leave again. But then I turned back. "You know, Ferdy—I mean Mr. Ferdinand—maybe I can find that book. I can ask around. Maybe somebody has it. Maybe somebody is reading it right now."

"Yes, someone may be reading it right now. You might be right!" He looked thoughtful. "Say, I like 'Ferdy.' Maybe you kids can call me Ferdy from now on?"

If he only knew! "Well, okay. I mean, it seems a little disrespectful. But if you insist!"

"I insist! And we'll find that book!"

"Yes, we will."

We shook hands and I left. It was weird. He'd probably be awake all night searching the Internet for books about South American girl basketball players. But that was him, I was me, and I knew what I had to do. I hurried home, passing right by the comics store. I went to my room, sat down at my desk, picked up a pencil, and started writing: "There was this amazing girl in the Andes Mountains. Her name was Angela, a rare beauty with emerald green eyes."

—⁓—

Binah Summary

The biblical story in this section describes Abraham and Sarah as very, very old. The great pain of their lives has been their inability to have a child. In the ancient world, this was considered the worst of all misfortunes. It signified that God was against you in some very basic way. Despite this, God had promised Abraham that he would be the founder of a great nation! This seemed to be a very deliberate and painful joke!

Then, out of nowhere, three men appear at Abraham's tent. Abraham immediately recognizes them as divine beings—angels. But if Sarah also sees this, she is in no mood to give them the respect that they deserve. And from a human perspective, why should she? Since God has treated her so badly, she does not see any reason why she should be nice to his messengers. In short, Abraham understands the angels' visit as another test that God has called on him to pass. Sarah sees it as an opportunity to feel bitterness and perhaps self-pity. While Abraham greeted the angels with kindness, Sarah remained inside the tent and out of sight.

But then an extraordinary thing happened. Because of the respect shown by Abraham, they have something very important to tell Sarah: finally, a son will be born to her and Abraham. Best of all, they don't just say, "It's going to happen someday." They say exactly when it's going to happen.

Despite her age, Sarah's response to this good news is very much like that of a teenager in the twenty-first century. When the angel tells Sarah that she'll give birth to a son within a year, she laughs—just as you might laugh if your father walked into your room and declared, "Well, I predict you're going to get all A's next term!" Or if your mother said, "If you apply to Harvard, I know you'll get in! Trust me!"

Whenever people act as if they have the power to see not just the future but your future, the tendency is to disbelieve them. Whenever someone—especially an older person—says, "You'd better listen to me because this is what's going to happen," your first impulse is probably to do the opposite. The truth is, sometimes you're right to do the opposite. But sometimes it can be very costly to ignore the understanding of another person, even if that understanding sounds like just another bit of advice.

CHAPTER NINE

Chochmah

The Power of Wisdom

Of all the qualities human and spiritual we've discussed in this book, only one has no "downside risk." We've seen, for example, that it's possible to be too kind or too judgmental or too focused on success and achievement. We've seen that what's positive in one environment can be negative in another context. But Chochmah, or wisdom, is different. *Wisdom is always good. It's impossible to have too much wisdom.*

One problem remains, however. Even when we understand how desirable it is to possess great wisdom, we still need to know what wisdom actually is—and it's not something that's easily put into words. A Kabbalistic proverb can provide a bit of quick help in this regard. "Who is wise?" asks the proverb, and then it answers, "He is wise who learns something from everyone." This is inspiring—it shows that wise people are also humble, but it still doesn't tell us what wisdom really is.

The truth is, nowhere in all the teachings of Kabbalah is there a definition of wisdom. Instead, we are given instructions on how to recognize wisdom in others and thereby to cultivate it in ourselves. The Zohar refers to fourteen specific qualities of a wise person. Some of these are quite technical and deal with strict observance of prayers and rituals, but the first five can have clear relevance to our everyday lives.

The first principle is to live in awe of God. We've discussed the concept of awe in connection with the Sefirah of Hod. It's the energy and power that comes from being in the presence of something much greater than yourself, and it's also the ability to transmit that energy to others. As our wisdom grows, we begin to experience this sense of awe, not just when we're facing an overwhelming spectacle—the Grand Canyon, for instance—but even when we're looking at things that others might consider quite ordinary. The Kabbalists tell us that whoever loses this sense of awe will be unable to connect with any other aspect of wisdom.

Love of God is the second principle of wisdom, and the defining quality of this love is the fact that it is unconditional. This is the way that God loves us, and to love him we must mirror that unwavering energy. God's love for us is not dependent on what we give him or do not give him. In fact, God cannot receive anything from us—he has already "got" everything. In the same way, God has given us the tools and teachings of Kabbalah, which enable us to overcome any challenge. At every moment, God gives us everything we need. A wise person understands this and loves God unconditionally in return.

The third principle is keeping an ongoing awareness of God's presence alive, whether through prayer or meditation. Or perhaps just focusing attention on the miracles that take place every moment.

Recognizing the unity of all things is the fourth characteristic of wisdom. Kabbalah teaches that all sense of fragmentation and disunity in our lives are illusions caused by the limitations of our perception and our awareness. The belief that chaos is reality is the most potent tool of the negative side of our being.

Finally, the fifth principle is the study of Kabbalah itself, just as you are doing right now as you read these words. But remember: study in the Kabbalistic sense encompasses all of life, not just intellectual activity. We study Kabbalah whenever we give of ourselves to another person or to any living thing. In this way, we add to our wisdom and draw positive energy into our lives.

—m—

*Adam, the first man, was granted supreme wisdom in the Garden of
Eden. He saw the future in the present. He saw the far end of the
universe from the very beginning. He was given God's own wisdom.
At that moment, Adam looked ahead and saw you, as you are today.
Now, in order to connect to the wisdom that Adam was given, you
must learn to look back and see him.*

Adam's Vision

When God created Adam in the Garden of Eden, He collected earth
from all over the world to form Adam's body. Then he mixed it with
water from all the oceans. So Adam was not just the first human
being in the whole world. He was also the whole world formed into
the first human being.

Before He breathed life into Adam's form, God did something
very wonderful and important. He revealed the entire future of the
universe to Adam—everything that was ever going to happen—and
it was all wonderful. There were no wars or epidemics, there was no
pain and suffering, and there were no evil people whatsoever. In
fact, there were no people who were anything less than truly joyful,
completely fulfilled, deeply spiritual human beings. It was a genuine vision of paradise on earth, forever.

Why did God disclose this vision to Adam? It was to make Adam
aware of everything that depended on his staying free from sin.
Adam was created perfect, and he needed to remain perfect in order
for the future of the world to be perfect as well. Unfortunately,
Adam and Eve ate the forbidden fruit, and the future of the world
became much more complicated. Instead of being a paradise in its
own right, the world became like a maze that we must navigate in
order to re-enter paradise under our own power. Instead of being a

simple statement of eternal truth, our lives became a coded document that we must learn to read.

The power to see the future that was granted to Adam was simply the very same power that constitutes the wisdom of God. It was the power to see what is going to happen through what is happening right now. This is what was given to Adam before his entrance to the world, and it was certainly a remarkable gift. As Adam discovered, we can change the vision for good or for bad, but you might ask, "How can I change it if I never got it in the first place." Yet Kabbalah teaches that the same gift that was granted to Adam comes to each of us before our birth.

Here's how it happens. When it is time for someone to be born, God already knows the identity and the true nature of that person, just as he knows this about everyone who has ever lived or who ever will live. Therefore God calls out to one of his angels that he should bring forth the soul of the person who is about to enter the world, and he speaks that person's name.

Then the soul is brought forth. Always and without exception the soul pleads with God to be spared having to enter the world. When this happens, God informs the soul that living in the world presents a great opportunity, one that can never be found even in the Upper World.

Then God directs an angel to show the soul the special place in heaven that is reserved for those who led truly righteous lives. In Hebrew, these are known as the tzaddikim. "These perfect men and women entered the world with the same reluctance that you feel now," the angel tells the soul. But because they observed God's commandments throughout their lives, they now have everlasting joy and fulfillment and can achieve the same exalted status by following the precepts of the Bible during their life on earth.

Having spoken those words, the angel then teaches the entire Bible and all its meanings to the soul, and this takes only a single instant. In just the blink of an eye, the soul becomes as wise in the ways of

God as any person does who ever lived. But that's only the beginning. The angel then takes the soul on a journey through time in which all the events of the soul's life on earth are made visible. The soul sees where it will be born, all the places it will live, all the people it will meet, and all the actions it will perform—and finally, it sees the grave in which it will be buried. Then the soul is placed in the womb of the woman who will become its mother.

When the day arrives for the soul's actual birth as a human being, the angel reappears to bring this about. Then the soul always protests just as strongly as it did when God first called it forth. But the angel reminds it that just as you have acquired a physical form against your will, now you will be born against your will. Someday, too, you will die against your will. You have already seen this with my help, just as with my help you have acquired the entire Bible in a single instant. You gained the power to see the future in the present, and in this sense you became One with the God. But now you must lose that wisdom as the price of entering the world. But you do not have to lose it forever. By learning God's teachings once again and by living in accordance with them, you can become truly wise during your lifetime. More important, you can take your place among the tzaddikim in heaven when your life on earth is done. With that, the angel touches the lips of the soon-to-be-born boy or girl, and everything that had been seen and learned is at once erased. This happened to *you*, just as it has happened to everyone who has ever been born. Infinite wisdom was given to you, along with the opportunity to regain it on your own.

Wisdom is something that's often found when you're looking for something else. The most profound insights, for example, can be gained from the most unlikely people: "Who is wise? The person who learns from everyone."

On the Road

The summer after high school ended, I got a job driving a taxi. Out where I lived, there were just malls and tract houses. Not much need for taxis, so I had a lot of time to think while I drove around, and I needed some time to think. I had worked every summer since I was in grade school, and I had saved every penny to help pay for college. But did I really want to go to college? Just getting in had been a huge hassle, and for what? I had never been what you would call a star student. What if I flunked out? I would hate that, especially if going to college was just something that my parents had talked me into doing.

Driving around in the cab, I thought about what I'd really like to do in the fall: hitchhike across America! I had been reading *On the Road*, by Jack Kerouac. I didn't really expect to like that book—it was written about fifty years ago—but the title seemed kind of cool, so I picked it up. Nothing really earthshaking. Just some guys traveling around. But they have a lot of adventures, they meet girls, and, the main thing is, they always seem really excited about whatever is going on. That's the feeling I'd like to have.

Even though I'm not totally great in school, I'm not against books and reading. In fact, I like to write poems and songs of my own. My dream life would be to travel around and write a book of poems and maybe get it published. Or I could hook up with a band and get them to do some of my songs. It was possible. No reason I couldn't do it. But would I have the guts to tell my parents that I didn't want to go to college? I wondered about that all summer while I was driving the cab.

To get a license as a taxi driver, I had to go to the police station and be photographed, be fingerprinted, and have my record checked for any crimes I might've committed. You would've thought that I was going to be an astronaut. But what I actually did all day was drive old people back and forth to their doctors' appointments.

Sometimes they even asked me to park and wait for them outside, but I didn't like to do that because they could be in there for hours. I didn't want to keep the meter running, but I didn't want to turn it off either.

Usually I told them that I had another fare on the radio, but that was hardly ever true. I would just drive around some more, or sometimes I would park and read the newspaper or read *On the Road* again. Sometimes I would even sleep.

I always kept the radio on when I was parked, and every couple of hours I would actually get a call. Then one day something really strange happened, although it started out like nothing unusual at all. The radio squawked, and I was directed to pick up a fare at one of the medical office buildings. I knew what that meant: another old person needed a ride home. And that's exactly what it turned out to be.

It was a doctor's office in a strip mall. I pulled up in front, and there was a tiny, frail woman standing there. She had one of those walkers that old people use, and she was holding onto it real tight, like she was afraid the tiniest breeze might blow her away. Maybe it would have! Anyway, I got out and helped her into the cab, and she gave me an address about five minutes away.

We started off. All of a sudden she said, "I never thought it would be like this." It kind of startled me, because for an old person her voice sounded pretty young and strong. With some of these people, you can hardly hear them—and most of them don't talk at all.

I knew what she meant, of course. "You mean, you never thought you'd be—like, sick?"

"I never thought I'd be old."

I wasn't sure what to say. But when I thought about it for a minute, it made sense. I mean, I didn't really think I would ever be old either, standing out in front of a doctor's office holding onto a walker. But maybe it could happen. It was one of those things that you had to believe in your mind, even if you couldn't really feel it in your gut.

"Yeah, I know what you mean," I said.

"You do?" She sounded surprised—like, how could I possibly know?

"Well, I think so. I mean, I never thought I was going to graduate from high school. When I was a freshman it seemed so far away. But now it's happened." It sounded funny when I said it. Here I was telling this person who has lived eighty or ninety years about how I felt four years ago. But she seemed to understand it the right way.

"Well," she said after a minute. "You've got your whole future in front of you."

"I guess that's right."

"So do I."

It blew me away when she said that. I mean, how much longer could she possibly live? In fact, I was a little worried that she might die right there in the cab. But who knows what goes through these old people's minds. So I didn't say anything, and just kept my eyes on the road. The ride only took a couple of minutes to get to her house.

It was a small one-story house like all the others on that street. I knew there were some young families around because a few of the houses had basketball nets in the driveway, but I knew there were many old people too. Most of them had somebody that stayed with them, like a nurse or something, but this woman seemed to be by herself. I was a little worried about her, but at least she lived until I pulled the cab into her driveway. Then I helped her use the walker to get to the front door.

"Have a good day," I said.

"Yes. Thanks for your help." She handed me a folded bill. "Keep the change."

"Great. Thanks."

"You've got your whole future ahead of you," she said again.

"Yes."

"But I wouldn't trade my future for anybody's." Then she smiled. Whoa. I helped her unlock her door and I got back in the cab. It freaked me out when she said that about her future. But why? She just meant she was ready to go, I guess. Or who knows? Maybe she meant she was going on a trip to see her grandchildren or something. Anyway, by the time I was out of the driveway, she was inside, her door was closed, and it was as if she had never been there in the first place.

But that was really only the beginning. I pulled out into the street, and a few doors down there was this guy standing at the curb. If anything, he looked even older than the old lady did. But he was also dressed in a completely different style, like he was a farmer or something. He was wearing overalls, and he was actually wearing a straw hat.

I slowly pulled up in front of him. "Hi," I said.

"Hi there!"

"Waiting for a tractor? Or, I mean, a cab?"

He laughed loudly. "Hey, that's a good one! And you know, I am waiting for a cab. I sure enough am."

"Well, come in."

We started off. I made eye contact in the rearview mirror. "Where are you going?"

"Greyhound bus station! Know where that is?"

"Sure."

"That's good. That's real good."

He seemed so happy. Many of these people seem sick and depressed, but this guy looked great. But there was also something strange about him. What was he doing standing out on that deserted street waiting for a cab?

"Did you call for a taxi?" I asked.

"Did I call? Nope."

"Well, how long were you waiting?"

"Not long. I just got out there, in fact."

"But you could have waited for hours before a cab came down that street. Maybe a week even."

"But here we are!"

"Yep."

"Yep!"

We drove along. All of a sudden he said, ""What's on your mind, son? Thinking about girls?"

I decided to play along. "Yeah! I just picked up this totally beautiful chick. Blond hair, blue eyes, she had it all. Love at first sight! I would have followed her anywhere. Maybe we could have gone out to California together on motorcycles, or maybe even to Alaska."

I could see him grinning in the mirror. "She sounds great. Did you get her name?"

"Her name? Yeah—Ashley."

"Ashley! That's a very attractive name!"

We both laughed. This guy was great! I could tell he was the kind of guy who had done many different things in his life. Maybe he'd been in the army, maybe he'd been a boxer, maybe he'd been married a couple of times and had kids. And now he was a farmer? I wanted to ask him about all this stuff. For some reason I felt really interested in him. The bus station was about ten minutes away. What should I ask him about first?

But then he said, "You worried about your future, son?"

He really surprised me. "What?"

"You worried about what you're gonna do? A lot of young fellows are."

"Yeah. Maybe a little. I'm trying to decide if I ought to go to college or not."

"Hm. Why wouldn't you want to go to college?"

"Well, I'm not really that into books."

"Hm. Hm. I've learned a lot from books."

"Really?"

"You find that hard to believe?"

"No. Not at all. It's just that you look more like a—working man."

He nodded and grinned. "More like a working man than a reading man, is that right?"

"That's what I meant. Anyway, there are some books that I like a lot. Maybe it's teachers that I'm not so wild about."

"Oh, is that it?" He seemed to be thinking about this. "I learned a lot from teachers too."

I didn't want to argue with him. I just drove for a while. I wanted to talk with him, but now I wasn't really sure where to start. I looked in the mirror again.

"I learned a lot from books. I learned a lot from teachers. But I learned the most from my problems," he said.

"Really?"

"That's right. And the harder they were, the more I learned."

Now I could see the bus station up ahead, with the Greyhound sign on the roof. Where could this guy be going on the bus? He looked like somebody who could be going almost anywhere. Maybe there was only one place I could be sure he wasn't going. He wasn't going to college.

I pulled the cab up to the curb. He handed me a folded bill. "Keep the change," he said.

"Thanks!"

He opened the door, grunted, and started to get out. For some reason I felt as if I wanted—needed—to say something to him; I felt like it was my last chance. But what could I say? And now he was out of the cab.

I jumped out of the driver's seat and called to him over the hood. "Excuse me. Mister—"

He turned. "What is it, son?"

"Uh, could I ask where you're going?"

He shrugged. "Anywhere, really. I'm just going."

Just going! Incredible! The way he said it sounded magical. "I'd give anything to do that!"

For the first time, he looked puzzled. "But you are just going." Then he laughed. "You're driving a taxi, aren't you?"

I sighed. "Yeah, I guess so." As I glanced up the street, I could see delivery trucks, soccer moms in their SUVs, and a school bus blocking traffic while it tried to make a turn. "But I'm not going where I want to go."

"How do you know that?"

The words came pouring out. "Because there's nothing to do here. Everybody does the same thing every day. We all went to the same school, and now we're all going to the same college. We'll all get the same kinds of jobs, we'll all have the same families, and eventually—eventually we'll all be buried in the same cemetery. I want to see new places. I want to meet different people."

"Well, you met me, didn't you? And you met me right here. If you had been someplace else—if you were up in the Rocky Mountains or out on the ocean—that wouldn't have happened, would it?"

He was looking straight at me with this incredibly powerful gaze. "No, I guess that's right," I said.

"And you know what else? You wouldn't have met—Ashley!"

He broke into a huge grin. I couldn't help but smile back. "Yeah, I wouldn't have met her. Definitely not!"

"You see? So what are you waiting for? You've got a great future ahead of you. Get back in that taxi cab, son. Get on the road."

—〰—

Chochmah Summary

The ancient Kabbalists defined wisdom in just a very few words, but as we'll see, there's a big difference between a definition and a true explanation. Very simply, wisdom is the power to see the future. But this doesn't mean looking into a crystal ball or traveling in a time machine. It's just a matter of knowing the forces and energies that are at work at a certain time and place and seeing how they're going to work themselves out.

Acquiring wisdom is one of the most important purposes of our lives. And it's not as difficult as you might think. Believe it or not, to a certain degree you are able to see into the future right now. This isn't something you were born with. It's an ability you've acquired through the experience of living in the world—and you can acquire more and more of it. In fact, the only limits on your potential wisdom are those you impose on yourself.

For example, when you were a small child, what did you "see" when you held a tiny seed in your hand? Obviously, your eyes saw nothing but a single, very small object. Just as important, your imagination also "saw" nothing more than the little round shape in the palm of your hand. But today you can look at a seed and easily visualize a fully grown tree. Although you may not know exactly what takes place biologically, you have no trouble accepting the concept that somehow an enormous object is already present in this much smaller one. Actually, this is wisdom. As you look at the seed, you're aware of the forces that are present inside it, and you know the result that those forces will bring about.

A seed, of course, is a material object. It's relatively easy to connect with changes that take place on the physical level. Wisdom becomes more complicated when we apply it in areas of emotion or spirituality. It might happen, for instance, that two of your friends start dating. Perhaps, it seems very clear to you that these two people are "wrong for each other"—that there may be a temporary attraction, but that things can't possibly work out. You may feel completely confident about this prediction, but you may also find that the growth of relationships is more complicated to foresee than the growth of seeds.

There are many, many more areas in which wisdom becomes increasingly complicated and increasingly important. What classes should you take—art, English, or biology? What college should you go to, or should you go to college in the first place? Who should you marry, or should you get married at all? For these kinds of questions, it's very difficult to act wisely without the benefit of experience. Could you possibly know that a seed would turn into a tree if you had never seen the process take place? In order to understand what was going to take place, you had to acquire information over a period of time. You had to see seeds, young trees, and fully grown trees that were now producing seeds of their own. At some point you probably even needed someone to explain the connections, or, perhaps, you read an explanation in a book. In any case, the wisdom you gained was a combination of your own experience and the experience of others that in one form or another was shared with you.

This multidimensional process of acquiring wisdom has some important lessons in itself. It teaches us (or should teach us) to be cautious about trusting our own judgment in things that are new to us. This isn't always easy to do. As you grew from childhood to teenager, you learned a lot. It's easy to assume that you've learned more than you really have. In fact, it's not at all difficult to feel like you've learned everything. That's an understandable mistake, but it's also a big one!

There's a better course to follow, and it splits the difference between assuming you know nothing and believing you know everything. These are two very powerful temptations, and Kabbalah teaches that it's important to resist both of them. As your life gets more complicated, there may be times when you wish it could be as simple as it used to be. A good way to do this is to go back into the role of a young child, when others made most of the decisions for you. As long as that was true, you didn't have to take any responsibility if something went wrong. After all, it wasn't you who made the decision. By making yourself completely dependent on other people, you may miss out on some very good things, but at least you have somebody else to blame for whatever bad things come along. Very simply, you receive both the benefits and the drawbacks of a baby-like existence.

At the other extreme, instead of telling the world that you're completely dependent, you present yourself as completely independent. There's a good chance you may even actually believe this! As both your body and your mind grow stronger, you may think there's nothing that can hurt you, nothing you can't understand, and nothing you shouldn't try. The evidence for this can seem very, very convincing. But if you act on it, you're definitely not acting wisely, and you may also be taking some very big and very unnecessary chances.

Let's put it this way. If wisdom is an ability to "see," the opposite of wisdom is a kind of blindness. Specifically, it's a blindness to where we really are in the world—and if we don't know where we are now, how can we fulfill the definition of wisdom, which includes seeing where we're going to be?

In the preceding story, the taxi driver is someone who wants very badly to be somewhere else, doing something other than what he's doing right now or other than he's going to be doing in the near future. He doesn't want to be in a boring suburb driving around in a cab all summer, and he's not sure whether he wants to go to college in the fall. Of course, he's not where he wants to be either, but he's prepared to let that take care of itself. "Anywhere but here" pretty much describes how he feels.

But then an interesting thing happens. He meets a man who is at a very different point in life—a man who perhaps has been to many of the places and has done many of the things the taxi driver would like to see and do. He doesn't tell the driver that it's wrong to want to have adventures or to go "on the road." Instead, he suggests that the driver is already on the road. He just needs to recognize that fact. That sounds simple enough, but it's not always easy to do, and it's not even easy to hear about.

For many young people—though not all—listening to advice from parents, teachers, or anyone over the age of thirty is a huge bore. To a certain extent, this is what nature intended, because it's important for all human beings to try new things and to make discoveries on their own. On the other hand, listening to older people can also save a lot of time and trouble!

Kabbalah teaches that everyone will eventually gain great wisdom. It may take a long time. It may even take more than one lifetime. But there'll come a day when every soul, including yours, possesses God's power to see the future in the present. There're two ways to arrive at that point. One way is through experience—that is, learning "the hard way" that if you put your hand on the hot iron, you're going to get burned. The other way is much easier and faster, but it requires a much higher degree of awareness and control. This second path to wisdom is through the teachings of Kabbalah. This second path will definitely make you a "better person," but that's not really what's most important right now. The important thing is that Kabbalah can save you a lot of time and trouble on the way to becoming the person you were intended to be. But you have to understand that and act accordingly.

The wisdom we have been discussing expresses itself in the world as the Sefirah of Chochmah. This is the highest form of spiritual energy available to us in the physical dimension. Only one level exists above this one. It is the Sefirah known as Keter, or crown—the final topic we'll discuss in this book.

#

CHAPTER TEN

Crown

So far we've focused on Kabbalistic principles and spiritual tools that can bring happiness into your life. Now, in closing, we'll look at what you can do to bring happiness into the lives of others, and why Kabbalah teaches that this is not just a great opportunity, but also a great responsibility.

It begins with the realization that your best interests can't really be separated from the best interests of everyone around you, and there's a story that illustrates this point really well. A group of people took a boat out into the middle of a lake to go fishing. Everyone was suddenly shocked to see that one of the fishermen was drilling a hole in the floor of the boat. "Are you crazy? What are you doing?" they all shouted at him. But the fisherman seemed very calm and just kept on drilling. "Don't worry," he said. "I'm not bothering you. I'm not drilling holes everywhere, just under my own seat."

The point of this story, of course, is that we are most definitely all in the same boat. This is a basic teaching of Kabbalah, and we need not only to understand it but also to put it into action in every way we can. Happiness isn't just getting what you want. It's also sharing that experience with everyone around you.

Why is this so important? Why isn't it enough for people to just enjoy the fruits of their labors and let other people solve their own problems? Why do we have to become good teachers and leaders as well as good followers and students?

The answer to that question is one of the most important of all Kabbalistic teachings. To understand it, try to imagine that you're at the beach building a sand castle—a pyramid made of sand that you want to be as tall as possible. First, you build the pyramid from the bottom up, and then you start adding small amounts of sand to the top in order to make it taller. But as you do this, you also know that eventually you won't be able to add any more without the whole pyramid collapsing. In fact, there will be a time when even adding one more tiny grain of sand will bring change to the whole shape of the pyramid. Just that single tiny addition will alter everything.

Kabbalah teaches that the situation of humanity in the world is very much like that pyramid. Whenever anyone performs an act of real giving and sharing, another grain of sand is added to the top of the castle, and we never know when even one more addition will cause the whole shape to change forever. Every human being has a responsibility for trying to be that last grain of sand that shifts the paradigm of all humankind. Each of us has a responsibility, not only to get happiness for ourselves, but also to bring about the transformation of the world. And as our influence becomes greater as our prosperity grows, our responsibility becomes greater too.

Do you feel you're not suited to be a leader? Moses felt the same way! When God called on him to lead the people out of slavery in Egypt, Moses was frightened. He is one of the greatest leaders in all of history, yet he was extremely hesitant to undertake the role that God wanted for him.

Moses actually argued with God about this for seven full days. He said, "Who am I that I should go to Pharaoh?" He was sure that someone else could do a better job of liberating the slaves. Moses even pointed out that he had a speech impediment, which would hardly make him an effective communicator before the world's most powerful leader.

Whenever you sense a weakness in yourself—especially a real weakness—recognize the opportunity to turn that weakness into strength. Kabbalah explains this principle in very straightforward terms. Whenever there is an opening on the spiritual level, whenever there is an empty space, whenever there is a vacuum—that empty space will be filled. But what will it be filled with? There are only two possibilities: it will be an opening for negativity or for doing the will of God, which is nothing other than happiness for you and everyone. And the choice is always yours. We make the choice through our own consciousness. If we choose to say, "This is not something I'm good at, so I'll back away from it," we are denying the power of the Light and inviting chaos and negativity into our lives.

—\\\\—

Kabbalah teaches that nothing is more to be desired than closeness to God. But how much would you be willing to give up in order to achieve that closeness? Many people try to hedge their bets. They want to study Kabbalah, but they don't want to change their lives in order to gain Kabbalah's wisdom and power. Deciding what to do about this can be very difficult, but sometimes God provides some help.

Every Loss Is a Gain

Once a very ambitious businessperson came to a great sage of Kabbalah for advice. The businessperson said, "There's an exciting deal that I could get involved in, but I'm not sure if I should do it. It's a chance to make a lot of money, but there's also risk involved. I know you're a scholar and a teacher rather than a businessperson, but do you think you could give me some advice?"

The Kabbalist said he would try, so the man described the business deal and waited to hear whether he should put money into it.

The sage thought for a moment. Then he said, "Yes, I think you should definitely take part in this investment. But you should also pray for God to guide you."

The businessman said that he would do just that, and then he left. But a few weeks later he reappeared, and he didn't look very happy. "I did as you said," he told the sage. "I put a great deal of money into the investment I told you about, and I also prayed for God to guide me. But I lost every penny!"

The great sage looked concerned. "Have you lost everything you had?" he said.

"Not quite everything," the businessperson said. "I still have some money in my savings. But I'm certainly less well off than I was before."

"Are there any other investment opportunities you could get involved with?"

The businessperson considered this question. "There are always investment opportunities coming along. But I'm a little reluctant after what happened last time. Do you really think I should take any more chances?"

"Absolutely," the sage said. "If there seems to be a worthwhile investment, you should definitely take part in it. Pray for guidance also."

So the businessperson departed. But a week or so later he returned, and he looked more miserable than ever.

"I went into another investment and I lost everything," he told the sage. "I prayed for guidance, but I guess my prayers were unanswered because now I don't have a penny to my name."

"Really?" the sage asked. "You lost all your money? Well, what about your house and your car? You still have those, don't you?"

The businessperson shook his head sadly. "I mortgaged my house and I sold my car to go into this investment. And now I have nothing left."

"Nothing?" asked the sage once again—and the businessperson was surprised to see that the sage looked strangely happy about it.

"That's right, I have nothing left. Not one penny," the businessperson said. "And by the way, what are you smiling about?"

The sage put his arm around the businessperson's shoulder. "I'm smiling," he said, "because now you can pray from the bottom of your heart. Now you can pray with nothing held in reserve. Now you can really merit the guidance you seek, because there's nothing left for you to do on your own."

—⁂—

Connection with the energy Keter is not something that you can plan to achieve. But that energy is present whenever you do something beyond what your highest expectations of yourself are. The key to making that happen is simply putting yourself in situations that can take you outside your comfort zone. That's what Moses did when he undertook to lead the people of Israel out of Egypt—and on a smaller scale, that's what happens to the girl in the following story.

Mistakes Will Happen

It's strange to think of studying as a sport, but that's what studying became over the past year for me and the other members of our school's academic decathlon team. Two mornings each week, we met in the school library for an hour before classes started. Month after month, we worked on our skills in the ten subjects of the competition. For us, it was more than just a game. It was a responsibility to represent our school in the things that school was really supposed to be all about. The purpose of school, after all, wasn't really supposed to be football or basketball. It was supposed to be about learning English and history and math. That's why the academic decathlon seemed almost like a sacred mission to us.

As I entered the library that morning, I fully expected to see the faces of my teammates streaked with tears. But they looked just the same as usual, with some bent over their books while others worked together on asking and answering questions. Well, I quickly realized there could be only one explanation. They had not found out yet what I had known for almost four days.

Mr. Sommers, our club director and faculty sponsor, had forgotten to turn in our paperwork for the regional academic decathlon tournament. Because I was the team captain, Mr. Sommers had personally told me about what had happened. He'd asked me not to inform the other team members because he felt that he ought to do that himself. But that had been last Friday, and now it was Tuesday morning. I thought he'd have told them by now because he'd certainly have seen all of them around the school, but apparently he'd decided to wait for the next regular meeting of the whole team.

Since I've been in high school, it's become obvious to me that kids see the teachers in very different ways. Some kids think the teachers are gods. They're intimidated by the teachers, they're frightened of them, and they'll do anything to keep them from getting angry. Usually it's either the really good students who feel this way—the ones who want to go to Harvard or Yale—or else the really weak students, who are scared of failing a class. Then there's the vast majority of kids who are somewhere in the middle academically. They usually have many other things on their minds, such as sports or social life. Instead of seeing the teachers as larger than life, they think the teachers are a kind of slightly sad official presence that you have to obey without paying too much attention. The teachers are like crossing guards to these people. You don't have to look at them, you don't have to talk to them, and you don't even have to think about them. If you just do what they want, even if it's done in a completely passive way, they let you alone and you can go on about your business. And the truth is, most of the teachers are completely comfortable in that role.

I have always been a little bit different, because I have never seen the teachers as larger than life or less than human. They're just people who are kind of in a tough spot. Except for the really young ones, who are just teaching for a couple of years until they go to law school or whatever, most of the faculty members aren't really suited to do anything else. They've gotten used to dealing with kids all the time, and they're kind of locked into it. Some of them are really good at it, but the hard part is that they don't really get a lot of respect from the rest of the world because they don't make a lot of money. So they seem slightly tired and depressed much of the time. As I said, most kids don't think about the real issues that the teachers are facing in their lives, but I've always done that, and it's made them a lot easier to understand.

Mr. Sommers was a perfect example of many of these issues. I knew he had four kids of his own, and supporting them couldn't have been easy on what teachers get paid. Our school is in a pretty upscale suburban community, and a lot of the kids just take money for granted. They have their own cars, they go on skiing vacations with their parents in the winter, and they assume that they'll never have to deal with the things that most people worry about every day. They just think about themselves all the time, because that's all they've ever learned to do. It's a little bit different with the kids on the academic decathlon team, but even they think that the school is like a shopping mall. The teachers are like salespeople standing behind the counters and hoping that you'll pay attention to them.

When it was obvious that the other kids hadn't yet heard about Mr. Sommers' mistake, I didn't say anything but just sat down at one of the library tables and waited for him to come in. I didn't have to wait long. He showed up just a few minutes later, and it was obvious he'd thought about just how he was going to handle this. His approach was "take the bull by the horns."

He said, "Well, I've got something to tell all of you, and I'm not proud of it. But here it is. I forgot to send in the papers for the regional tournament, and now the deadline is past. I know you've all worked really hard, and I don't have any excuses. If you want to quit the team or even disband the club, I will certainly understand.

So now I'll leave you alone to discuss this. Just let me know what you want to do, and whatever you decide will be fine."

Then he got up and walked out of the library. He was there for less than three minutes. But it wasn't because he didn't care about what had happened. It was obvious, to me at least, that he was really shook up about it. It was actually somewhat disturbing to see an adult caught in the situation that kids face all the time: you've done something wrong and now you have to explain it. Obviously Mr. Sommers had taken the "short and sweet" route, which was probably as good as any.

As soon as he left the library, I could see everybody was in shock. I tried to look like I was in shock too, even though I had already known about the mistake. I certainly had been in shock when I first heard about it. Anyway, there are ten people on the team and at least eight of them wanted to quit immediately. Actually, other tournaments were available that we could go to besides the regionals, but nobody seemed to be thinking about that. They all just kept threatening to quit and not even go to the events that we were already signed up for.

I certainly knew how they felt, but I was not as angry as everyone else was. Yes, I was upset that we could not compete in the regionals, but I was not about to quit over it. In fact, I felt that we really needed to come together as a team to get over the hurt and pain that we all felt. That's what I had tried to get across to Mr. Sommers when he first told me about his mistake. I wanted to call a special meeting of the team in which I would express my feelings, but he asked me not to do that. I thought it was because he wanted to talk to each kid individually, but apparently he had decided just to wait for the next regular meeting. Now, though, I really wanted to tell the other kids how I felt, which was probably a lot different from how they were feeling at that particular moment. In fact, I was afraid they would attack me in some way for trying to be positive when they were not finished being angry.

We were all sitting at the same table in the library. Everyone knew that in about ten minutes the bell was going to ring to start the regular school day, but they all wanted to vent as much as possible. It was hard to get a word in edgewise, but finally I saw my chance and I went for it.

"I know how everyone feels right now," I started, "and I know I am feeling the same anger and hurt that everyone else is. But I also want to say that we need to unite as a team and to put all the anger to the side."

They all looked at me as if I was a psycho, but I just kept talking. "We won't be able to be in the regional tournament, but we can still be in the other tournaments that we're already signed up for. Maybe we can even go to the national event if our record is good enough. Maybe they'll give us a special dispensation because Mr. Sommers forgot to send in the papers for the regionals."

While I was saying this, an amazing revelation came to me. I'm not a religious person, but I suddenly had this insight that what had happened to our academic decathlon team and Mr. Sommers was exactly what had happened to humanity in general in its relationship with God. What a startling leap—but it explained so much. People like to feel that they've been let down by an all-powerful father figure who was supposed to be taking care of them. If they can feel that way, it gives them a chance to assume the victim role, which is something many people are really eager to do.

"So what we really need to do from now on," I said, "because we know we're a good team, is to have a chance to prove it to the world. Who cares what's happened so far? It's what happens from now on that really matters."

Then I stopped. Had it sounded unbearably corny? Maybe so. I averted my eyes from the rest of my team, thinking that they would hate me for taking away the moment when they could feel sorry for themselves. Amazingly, however, one of my teammates spoke up in support of me, and soon everyone was talking and laughing. It felt so good to speak my mind and then get that support in return. Although I had been afraid, I faced those fears, and I think that helped everyone out of a very bad spot.

As it turned out, we ended up finishing well at the other tournaments we entered. At the end of the season we were 40th out of 200 teams in the nation. It wasn't good enough to be in the national tournament, so we didn't even have to ask for special consideration. We were proud of ourselves for pulling through the hard times and ending the season on a good note. I was proud of myself for facing my fears, and I felt rewarded when we completed the season. I was overjoyed that we were able to all pull together, even if we didn't finish on top. And I felt that I had been a leader, even if I didn't lead us into the Promised Land.

—⚭—

Keter Summary

The task of every person in the world is the same one that Moses faced. If you don't feel that you have the capabilities to be a leader and a teacher, consider what the Kabbalists tell us about Moses' speech impediment. It was not a liability. It was an opening through which he would receive the divine energy. Moses had an excuse, but his disability was really like the net on a tennis court. It may cost you some points, but you can't make any great shots without it!

Right now, let's look at three specific insights you can use to fulfill this final and most important prerequisite for Kabbalistic wisdom: First is the realization of the power that you have to lead others, because you have God's Light within you. In fact, you may never have thought about it, but you are probably already a leader and teacher to many people in your school and your family. Second, you can learn to turn a perceived weakness into a strength. You may have already done this in order to gain prosperity in your own life, and now you can use this ability to benefit others. The third insight focuses on the fact that you can receive more Light and strength when you have first done the maximum on your own.

In thinking about these things, remember that Moses was very aware of his weaknesses as someone who was going to confront the Pharaoh of Egypt. Moses could not speak well, and for years he had been living as a shepherd out in the desert. Now, with all his short-comings, he was going to take on the burden of freeing his people from a brutal tyrant.

How did he do it? The key was certainty that he was acting as an instrument of God. He had no stature or power on his own, but for the same reason he had no weaknesses or liabilities. He was the channel for the infinite energy of the Light. As a result there was no weakness he could not overcome in himself and there was no weakness in other people that he could not help them to overcome. And by leading others, he became stronger and more fulfilled himself.

Suppose someone were to ask you if you could lift a three hundred pound weight over your head. Unless you've been doing some serious training for the past few months, the chances are you wouldn't be very optimistic about your ability to do something like that. And why should you want to do it, anyway? Just because I asked you? That probably doesn't give you much motivation.

But what if there was an earthquake and someone you deeply cared about was trapped under a three hundred pound block of cement. Do you think you could lift that piece of rubble? One thing is for sure: you would certainly try it. You would certainly have a high degree of motivation. Even if it has been years since you lifted anything heavier than your CD player, you would try to move that three hundred pound weight. And if you saw yourself as an instrument of God at that moment, I guarantee that you would succeed.

Now let's extend that analogy a little further. Suppose instead of asking you to lift a weight, I were to ask you to take responsibility for sharing what you've learned in this book with three other people within the next week. And it wouldn't just be a matter of telling them about the contents of the book; it would involve really becoming a mentor and a model for three people in the creation of joy. You might say, "Well, that sounds like a very noble aspiration and I'll definitely think about it. But I'm really stressed. Let me get back to you."

But what would happen if you really knew in the depths of your soul that your own happiness depended on your furthering the happiness of other people? What would happen if you were absolutely certain that your future and the destiny of those you love depended on this? You would be right on it! It wouldn't be a matter of getting back to anybody next week! This is the kind of commitment we need to make in becoming teachers of joy and of Kabbalah as a whole. Because we are all in the same boat, we are all dependent on one another. We will only gain complete fulfillment as individuals when we have all gained it collectively as well.

Furthermore, if there was a certain aspect of this task that you felt you were weak in, you would just work harder to strengthen that area. Think of the example we used a moment ago, about lifting the heavy weight. If you knew that something tremendously important depended on your being able to lift a three hundred pound weight one week from today, you would not spend the next seven days lying on the beach. You would undertake some serious preparation. You would probably start lifting weights morning, noon, and night. In fact, the weaker you thought you were, the harder you would train. You would do everything in your power to turn your weakness into strength.

This is related to the third insight on becoming a leader and teacher. The tool consists of doing everything possible on your own because that's when you will get help from God. It's not just a matter of saying, "This is great. God wants to help me move the world toward happiness, so I'll just ask for help and it'll all get done." The old saying "Heaven helps those who help themselves" has a lot of truth to it. God desires to help you, but you also have to desire that help deeply. It has to be a necessity, not a luxury. Not only do you have to want the assistance of the Light, but you have to really want it. You have to need it with your whole being.

—⁂—

Kabbalah teaches that there is no place for punishment after we leave this world. There is no hell, there is no purgatory, and there is no Inferno where souls have to suffer for their sins. There is not even a court or tribunal where good deeds are weighed against our bad ones and judgment is handed down. Instead, we judge ourselves. And how does this happen? We are shown the full potential that our souls possessed. We are shown what we could have become in the world, and we must compare what was possible with what actually transpired.

Whether this will be a heavenly experience or a hellish one is really up to us—and we are making that choice at this instant. I hope that you choose happiness for yourself in every moment of every day, both by using the tools presented here and by sharing them with others.

Resources

Books

As Kabbalah becomes better known, more and more books have appeared on its teachings and traditions. Although far from a complete list, the tiles below represent some of the most authentic and most accessible material on the wide variety of Kabbalistic teachings and traditions. While you should feel free to explore them in any order you choose, the list below represents a natural progression from original sources to more modern and specialized commentaries.

Tanakh: The Holy Scriptures. Jewish Publication Society. Familiarity with the Bible is absolutely essential for understanding Kabbalah. And it's not called the "Good Book" for nothing!

The Zohar: Volumes One and Two. Translation and commentary by Daniel C. Matt. Stanford University Press. The publication of the first two volumes of the central text of Kabbalah is a milestone in the history of these teachings. Although the Zohar is a very difficult book to follow, these books—with their authoritative notes and introduction—can literally be read over the course of a lifetime.

The Legends of the Jews: From Joseph to the Exodus by Louis Ginzberg and Henrietta Szold. Johns Hopkins University Press. A great anthology of Bible stories with additional material from folk stories and fables. See everything that the Bible leaves out!

The Midrash Says: Volumes 1–5 by Rabbi Moshe Weissman. Benei Yakov Publications. This wonderful series combines Biblical verses with commentary, stories, and other related material. The traditional characters and settings are vividly brought to life.

The Essential Zohar by Rav P. S. Berg. Bell Tower Books. An introduction to the Zohar by a leading contemporary Kabbalist.

Honey from the Rock by Lawrence Kushner. Jewish Lights Publishing.

The Book of Letters: A Mystical Alef-Bait by Lawrence Kushner. Jewish Lights Publishing. Lawrence Kushner is both a rabbi and an extremely effective writer for young readers on Jewish mystical topics. His book on the Hebrew alphabet combines text and illustrations and a truly Kabbalistic style.

Teaching of the Jewish Mystics by Perle Besserman. Shambhala. This small anthology offers sayings of the great sages of Kabbalah, as well as from the Zohar and other original texts.

These Are the Words: A Vocabulary of Jewish Spiritual Life by Arthur Green. Jewish Lights Publishing. A dictionary of Hebrew words that are essential for understanding Kabbalah and Judaism as a whole.

Around Sarah's Table by Rivka Zakutinsky and Yaffa Leba Gottlieb. Jewish orthodox and mystical teachings imaginatively dramatized from a contemporary woman's point of view.

Web Sites

As with books, there are many Web sites on Kabbalistic topics. You can find them with any search engine. The sites below are excellent sources for books as well as for explanations of diverse Kabbalistic topics.

www.jewishencyclopedia.com. A huge resource of information on many subjects.

www.jewishvirtuallibrary.org. This site provides information on contemporary as well as traditional subjects.

www.kabbalah.com. The Web site of the Kabbalah Centre, an organization dedicated to bringing Kabbalistic teachings to everyone who desires to learn.

www.shamash.org. A very large online resource for books and other Jewish material.

www.jewishlights.com. An outstanding publisher of books on a variety of contemporary Jewish topics.

www.aronson.com. Books and stories that lay hidden for hundreds of years are now available from this publisher, and can be ordered online.

Bookstores

Here is a sampling of Jewish bookstores around the country, with phone numbers as available. There may, of course, be other stores in your area.

Arizona

Scottsdale Judaica
10211 North Scotsdale Road
Scottsdale, AZ 85253-1424
(480) 922-0250

California

Bodhi Tree Bookstore
8585 Melrose Avenue
West Hollywood, CA 90069-5199
(310) 659-1733

East West Bookstore
324 Castro Street
Mountain View, CA 94041-1206
(800) 909-6161

Living Torah Judaica
1130 Wilshire Boulevard
Los Angeles, CA 90017-1904

Connecticut

Judaica of New Haven
1454 Whalley Avenue
New Haven, CT 06515-1130
(203) 387-5816

Illinois

Rosenblum's World of Judaica
2906 West Devon Avenue
Chicago, IL 60659-1508
(773) 262-1700

Massachusetts

Israel Bookshop
410 Harvard Street
Brookline, MA 02446-2902
(617) 566-7113 or (800) 323-7723

Minnesota

Brochin's
4813 Minnetonka Boulevard
St. Louis Park, MN 55416
(952) 926-2011

New York

Eichler's
62 West 45th Street (betw. Fifth and Sixth Avenues)
New York, NY 10036
(877) EICHLER [342-4537]

and

1401 Coney Island Avenue
Brooklyn, NY 11230
(888) EICHLER [342-4537]

J. Levine Books & Judaica
5 West 30th Street
New York, NY 10001
(800) 553-9474 or (212) 695-6888

Judaica of Great Neck
107 Middle Neck Road
Great Neck, NY 11021-1219
(516) 482-4729

Quest Book Shop
240 East 53rd Street
New York, NY 10022-5201
(212) 758-5521

Washington

Seattle Judaica
4541 19th Avenue NE
Seattle, WA 98105-3301
(206) 527-6734

Index

DAT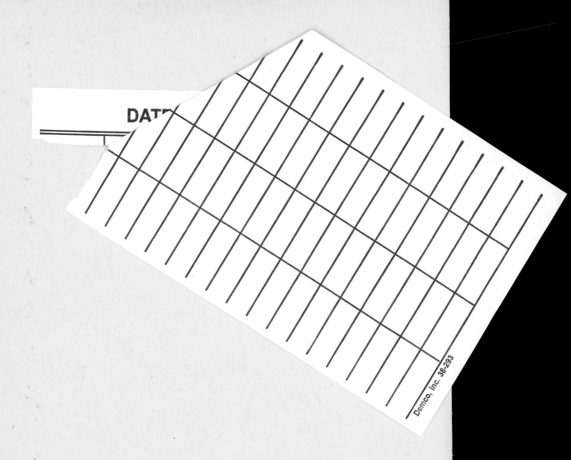

Demco, Inc. 38-293

The Tycher Library
in the
Mankoff Center for Jewish Learning

3JED000008584V